THE
CHRISTIAN FRAME
OF MIND

Thomas F. Torrance

1985

The Handsel Press

CONTENTS

PREFACE

My purpose in this book is to set before the reader some considerations regarding the distinctive contribution of the Christian mind to human life and thought, especially within the context of our knowledge of the world as it is steadily being transformed through the discoveries that modern science has been making about this vast universe of ours and the way nature everywhere behaves within it. As I have tried to show in *Divine and Contingent Order*, 1981, and in *Transformation and Convergence in the Frame of Knowledge*, 1984, the rise and development of our scientific culture has been much more influenced by fundamental Christian ideas than is commonly realised. Some very eminent thinkers like the late John Macmurray have even argued that science as we now pursue it is one of the principal products of the Reformation in the sixteenth century. I would not want to depreciate the impact of the Reformation, or of the Renaissance, upon the rise of modern science, for it was undoubtedly very considerable in this regard, although I believe that the roots of this influence go rather further back in the history of Christian thought. Certainly, the fact that science and theology do have common ground within our western tradition helps to explain why real dialogue is possible between Christian theology and natural science at the basic level of their controlling beliefs and concepts, without compromise on either side. On the other hand, the further dialogue of this kind is pursued, the clearer it becomes that theology and science have both critical and constructive contributions to make to each other, not least where they are so different from one another.

While some of the arguments in these earlier works are carried further here, in many respects this little book may be treated as an introduction to the more detailed and difficult discussion offered in them. All four chapters derive from lectures given on different occasions. The first was delivered before members of the Hellenic Societies in Britain in January, 1984, on the occasion of their celebration of "The Three Hierarchs", a festival in honour of three outstanding Fathers of the Church which Greek Institutions throughout the world hold each year. The second was given at the invitation of the University of Alberta at Edmonton in February, 1983, as part of their 75th birthday celebration, and was repeated at a local meeting of the American Scientific Affiliation held at Kinnewick, Washington, in March, 1983. The third lecture was prepared in response to a request from *The Calgary Institute for the Humanities,* in the University of Calgary, for a symposium devoted to 'the implications

3

of contemporary developments and discoveries in science for the uniqueness of man', in April, 1984. The fourth lecture was first given to the University of Edinburgh in 1977 and then, somewhat later, along with the second lecture in Edmonton in 1983. Since all four addresses had to do with the bearing of the Christian mind upon human culture, they "asked" to be put together in this way, although some repetition in thought and language was inevitably involved in their presentation. The first is to be found in a different form in *Texts and Studies* vol. III, 1984, published in London and Athens, while the main substance of the second has already appeared in a shorter form in *The Month*, December, 1983, published in London. I am grateful to the editors of these publications for their courtesy in agreeing to their appearance in the revised versions presented here.

I should like to dedicate this book to the Rev. Professor Emeritus David Cairns of the University of Aberdeen, to whose staunch friendship and wise help I have been greatly indebted for many decades.

Thomas F. Torrance
Edinburgh, April, 1984.

Chapter 1

THE GREEK CHRISTIAN MIND

I should like to take one principal theme from the teaching of three great Doctors of the Church, St Basil of Caesarea, St Gregory Nazianzen, and St John Chrysostom, and show how they combine to set the distinctive pattern of the Greek Christian mind which has so profoundly influenced our western tradition, not only in the Church but in the foundations of our scientific culture. To some people it may appear rather arbitrary to isolate one idea from each of these "Three Hierarchs", as they are traditionally called, and put them together in this way, but I believe that this procedure will have the effect of throwing into relief a sequence of thought latent in the "consensus of the Fathers" which is particularly relevant for us today.

St Basil of Caesarea

I should like to fasten upon a concept central to his great work the *Hexaemeron*, in which he offered to his contemporaries a Christian cosmology by way of interpreting the first chapter of the book of Genesis dealing with "the six days of creation". This is the concept of the creation of the whole universe in form and being out of nothing. All things visible and invisible, including man in mind as well as body, took their absolute origin from the free creative will of God. As the late Professor Georges Florovsky used to point out, this idea of the radical contingency of the universe and its inherent rational order was utterly alien and indeed quite unintelligible to the Greek mind. For classical Greek thought the universe was necessary and self-explanatory, eternally co-existing with God. The rational forms immanent in the universe which gave it its beautiful geometrical order were held to be divine, so that to speak of the universe as created in form and being out of nothing was regarded as an act of impious atheism. However, it was at this very point that the Greek mind came under the transforming impact of divine Revelation as it was mediated through Jesus Christ the incarnate *Logos* of God, through whom all things were made from nothing and by whom they are unceasingly sustained in their order and being.

Although the doctrine of the contingent nature of the creation was held by Christian thinkers from the very beginning, it had taken some time for the theologians of the Church to give it adequate expression in face of the

5

accepted concepts and language of Greek philosophy and science. It was above all to Athanasius that a clear Christian understanding of the creation of the world, including its space and time, was indebted. He achieved that in argument against Origen's notions of the eternal co-existence of the world with God and the pre-existence of rational souls, and in establishing against Arian heretics the fundamental principle that there is no community in being or likeness between the creature and God, for God is beyond all created being. Athanasius called in question the Greek concept of the *logos* as a cosmological principle and rejected the idea, which some earlier Christian thinkers had used, of 'seminal *logoi*' immanent in nature. He also showed that while man, unlike any other creature, had been made in the image of God, that image is properly to be understood in terms of grace (*he kat'eikona charis,* was his expression), and not in terms of any natural kinship with the divine. A radical distinction must be drawn between the uncreated Rationality of God and the created rationality with which man is endowed. The rational human being, together with the whole intelligible order of the universe of space and time, has been created out of nothing by God in the transcendent freedom of his love and will, although by the grace of God man has been given a distinctive place in the cosmos in the service of God's supreme purpose of love. For Athanasius, as for the great Nicene theology to which he contributed so masterfully, it was the Incarnation of the Son or Word of God that provided the central and controlling point for a Christian understanding of creation as well as redemption.

These were the basic theological insights which St Basil took over and developed in his own characteristic way in the *Hexaemeron.* In that work biblical teaching, and scientific convictions critically assessed from a theological perspective, were remarkably coordinated to provide the Church with the first coherent account of the created cosmos from a satisfactory Christian point of view. St Basil certainly made use of a number of scientific ideas, taken from contemporary textbooks on physics and astronomy, which are not acceptable to us today, but his cautious and critical handling of them, within a profound theological grasp of the relation of the creation to the transcendence of God, remains what Father George Dragas has called "a model for any work which tries to coordinate theological and scientific data".

My concern here is not to offer an account of St Basil's cosmology but to point out the significant part played by the *Hexaemeron* in the formation of the Greek Christian mind. Three ideas, in particular, need to be stressed.

First, St Basil considerably reinforced the concept of the contingent nature of the universe by showing that in its creation we must make room in our thought for a transcendent beginning beyond all material or

6

temporal beginning. The absolute origin of the universe is to be attributed to the free sovereign act of God the *Pantokrator*. That is not something we can reach through tracing back any process in the cosmos to its beginning, for even that beginning had a beginning beyond itself in God, which, in the nature of the case, we may know only through divine revelation. Thus by its very nature, St Basil argued, the cosmos is intrinsically *incomplete* — far from being self-sufficient or self-explanatory it is ultimately to be understood only from its contingence upon God.

Second, in commenting upon the Genesis account of creation through the majestic fiat of God: 'Let there be', St. Basil pointed out that though acts of divine creation took place timelessly, the creative commands of God gave rise to orderly sequences and enduring structures in the world of time and space. It was thus that the voice of God in creation gave rise to laws of nature. Expressed the other way round, this means that all the laws of nature, all its intelligible order, are to be regarded as dependent on the Word of God as their source and ground. Thus even physical law must be treated as a contingent form of order which is finally intelligible only as it points beyond itself to a transcendent ground of intelligibility in the *Logos* of God the Creator, for it is upon that ground that its constancy reposes. That is to say, it is the Word of God that constitutes "the cosmological constant", to use a modern expression.

Third, St Basil took over the Athanasian concept of "the grace of the image" that gives man his unique place in the cosmos in relation to God on the one hand and in relation to the physical creation on the other hand. Man is a creature who belongs in body and mind to the realm of contingent being, but he has been made to "look up" to God, and thus to be that rational constituent of the creation in whom the secret of its purpose in the loving providence of God is lodged. It is in and through man and his peculiar place in the cosmos, therefore, on the boundary between heaven and earth, the divine and the creaturely, the invisible and the visible, that its real destiny will be disclosed. God has given man a function in the world where he may discover things passed over in silence by Holy Scripture, provided that he observes the limits of the created order and realises that nothing in God's creation happens by mere chance.

Essential to this cosmological outlook lies the Christian concept of the radical contingence of the universe and its rational order. And central to all that is the conception, so impossible for the ancient Greeks, of the contingent nature of the human mind created by God out of nothing but given a unique relation to his own transcendent Mind through grace. The incorporation of those ideas in St Basil's *Hexaemeron* played a very important role, not only in challenging the intellectual foundations of the classical outlook upon the world of visible and invisible reality, but in helping to transform the Greek mind in a way that has left its mark upon the very basis of our western culture. Evidence for its far-reaching effect can be seen already in the fourth century in the *Hexaemeron* of St Ambrose of Milan, and especially in the *De Opificio Mundi* of John Philoponos, the first great Christian physicist, in sixth century Alexandria. But let me mention also two other works that reveal the influence of St Basil: the *Hexaemeron* of St Bede in the eighth century which left its mark upon the history of British thought; and the *Hexaemeron* of the remarkable Robert Grosseteste, Bishop of Lincoln in the twelfth century, in which we begin to see at long last the fruit of the Greek Patristic doctrine of contingence in the emergence of an empirical scientific approach to the understanding of the created universe.

St Gregory of Nazianzus

We turn now to the second of our three Hierarchs, "The Theologian", as he was deservedly called in the ancient Church, not least for his profound insights into the doctrine of the Holy Trinity. Incidentally, the second person to be accorded that title was John Calvin who had been so deeply influenced by St Gregory Nazianzen, and stood so close to him in his understanding of the Trinity that to be called 'The Theologian' was certainly not inappropriate.

The leading idea I have selected from Gregory Nazianzen's teaching derives from St Paul's Epistle to the Colossians in which he spoke of human beings as *alienated* from God and at *enmity* to him in their *mind*, but now as reconciled to him through the body and blood of Christ. A controversy had arisen in the Church over the conception of the divine-human Person of Jesus Christ advocated by Apollinaris of Laodicea, a friend of St Basil. Apollinaris wanted to avoid the idea that there was a double personality in Christ comprising a divine and a human person, which he thought could not be avoided if the Incarnation involved the union of a complete divine nature and a complete human nature. Moreover, in view of the fact that the human mind or the ruling element in human nature was fallen and necessarily imbued with evil, he wanted to avoid any idea that in his human nature Jesus was at enmity to God and in need of moral improvement. And so Apollinaris put forward the theory that the Son of God became man in Jesus Christ in such a way that his divine Mind or *Logos* replaced the human mind, while nevertheless taking to himself a living human body.

That idea was challenged at once as a heretical deviation from saving faith, notably by the author of two works *Against Apollinaris*, which Dr. G. D. Dragas has convincingly shown must be accepted as Athanasian, and by the two Gregories, Gregory of Nyssa and Gregory of Nazianzus.

8

They all insisted that such a conception of Incarnation and of Redemption was evangelically defective. If Jesus Christ did not have a full and complete human mind, then God had not really become man; moreover, if the principal and most needy part of human nature had not been assumed, then man's salvation is seriously wanting and still to be accomplished. It was Gregory Nazianzen's argument (in his first *Letter to Cledonius*) which was decisive. "If anyone has put his trust in Christ as a Man without a human mind, he himself is really bereft of mind, and quite unworthy of salvation. For that which he has not assumed he has not healed; but that which is united to his Godhead is also saved. If only half Adam fell, then that which Christ assumes and saves may be half also; but if the whole of his nature fell, it must be united to the whole nature of him who was begotten, and so be saved as a whole." This argument that "the unassumed is the unredeemed" had been put forward very early by St Irenaeus, who did so much to clarify and deepen the theological grasp of the Gospel in the second century, and was later powerfully reinforced by St Cyril of Alexandria in the fifth century.

This controversy in the Church had two far-reaching results. It established the doctrine that the manhood of the Lord, including his human mind, was complete; and it secured the fundamental conviction that in the Incarnation the holy Son of God assumed from the Virgin Mary our fallen human nature, with all its weakness, sin and guilt, yet in such a way that instead of sinning himself he brought the judgment of God to bear upon us in the depths of our human nature, redeeming, healing and sanctifying at the same time what he took from us, through his atoning birth, life, death and resurrection. The particular point on which I wish to fasten, however, is that it is above all in his inward rational human nature, in his *mind*, that man is fallen, distorted, and at enmity to God and his truth, so that it is above all in his *mind* that man needs to be redeemed and put in the right with God. It was at that very point that St Gregory Nazianzen made such a signal contribution to the Greek Christian mind. The Christian mind is not merely the mind that knows itself to be utterly contingent upon God, but the healed mind, the mind that is reconciled to God through the saving and sanctifying life and work of our Lord Jesus Christ.

It is unfortunate, and very astonishing, that Latin theology never really appreciated the profound implications of the Greek Patristic principle that "the unassumed is the unhealed". This western divergence from the Eastern Church can be traced back to Leo the Great's hesitation to accept the fact that in the Incarnation the Son of God took our depraved human nature upon himself, while redeeming, healing and sanctifying it in himself. He held instead that it was not our fallen Adamic nature but some neutral human nature in Christ that became the instrument for his saving work for mankind. The theological consequences of that position were immense, as we can see in the typical approach of Latin theology to the idea of original sin as in the teaching of St Augustine, in its formulation of a doctrine of atonement largely in terms of external juridical relations, and of course in the Roman dogmas of "the immaculate conception" and the "assumption of Mary", which remain a real barrier between the Eastern and Western Church. Apart from these specific doctrines, however, failure to recognise that the human mind, far from being neutral, is actually estranged and twisted, and thus in need of internal healing, opened the door to a pre-Christian Greek rationalism that has affected not only western theology but all western culture and science.

It is at this very point that the transformation of the Greek mind through Greek Patristic theology has so much to offer us today, not least in our great scientific struggle to match the operations of our human minds with the rational structures of the universe as created by God. Here let us link together the contributions to the Greek Christian mind which I have picked out from the thought of St Basil and St Gregory Nazianzen. I refer to St Basil's claim that the laws of nature are permanent features impressed upon the creation through the commanding Voice of God. As such they are to be regarded as open, contingent forms of order which derive their constancy from the Word of God and may ultimately be understood by us only as we are able to coordinate them with their source and ground in that Word of God. That is clearly not possible for people whose minds are alienated from God and at enmity with him. It is here, then, that we must take into account the insistence of St Gregory Nazianzen that in the Incarnation the Son of God took our depraved rational nature upon himself in order to heal and redeem it in himself, and thus reconcile our very minds to God in and through the birth, life, death and resurrection of Jesus Christ. And so the question must be asked: How far even in our scientific struggle to understand the rational order of nature, do we need to bring to it a redeemed and sanctified mind?

Let me recall, in passing, a striking point once made by the late Professor F. Gonseth, one of Europe's leading mathematicians. In a group of theologians and scientists the idea was put forward that in theology one cannot but be morally affected in one's deepest self through the kind of personal interaction with the living God that genuine knowledge of him requires, whereas in the exact or mathematical sciences which are strictly impersonal, that is not the case. One cannot be a genuine theologian without being good, whereas it is possible for an immoral person to be a good mathematician. Gonseth rejoined that one cannot be a good mathematician without a "sanctity of mind", if only

10

because the purity and precision of mathematical thinking are incompatible with any kind of mental dishonesty.

This is not at all an irrelevant issue in view of the problems that now face us in our scientific inquiries, especially as we push them to the very boundaries of being, whether in microphysical or in astrophysical dimensions. On the one hand, we sometimes find that we have to reckon with dark, disorderly and irrational elements in the universe which baffle us. And on the other hand, we have learned that there are what Michael Polanyi has called "destructive tendencies" in the human mind. In all basic scientific activity we rely upon a deep intuitive accord between the laws of our mind and the laws of nature, so that any disharmony in that relationship gives rise to 'noise' in the functioning of our minds, distorting the patterns of thought which we develop in our attempts to grasp the orderly structures inherent in the universe that God has created. Thus the deeper and the more refined our scientific research becomes, the more we need the sanctifying reconciliation of the human mind with the Word of God that is mediated to us through Jesus Christ. Some intersection of symmetries between the order of redemption and the order of creation seems to be called for. It is just here, then, if we are to follow out the implications of the teaching of St Basil and St Gregory Nazianzen, that deep-level coordination between theological and natural science should prove helpful.

St John Chrysostom

He is the last of our three Hierarchs, whose eloquent oratory has been rightly described as combining the Christian spirit with Greek beauty of form. To countless people through the centuries John Chrysostom has been associated with the liturgy that bears his name, although he was probably not responsible for it even in an earlier version of that which has come to be accepted for general use in the Greek Orthodox Church. In Britain, of course, John Chrysostom is remembered for his beautiful prayer incorporated by Thomas Cranmer in *The Book of Common Prayer*: "Almighty God, who hast given us grace at this time with one accord to make our common supplications unto thee; and dost promise that when two or three are gathered in thy Name thou wilt grant their requests: Fulfil now, O Lord, the desires and petitions of thy servants, as may be most expedient for them; granting us in this world knowledge of thy truth, and in the world to come life everlasting." While this particular prayer is mainly petitionary, certainly the sanctification of the human mind in the worship of God *for God's sake*, which is so characteristic of Orthodox worship, has continued to be the inestimable fruit of that liturgical tradition.

11

Be that as it may be, there are two distinctive ingredients in John Chrysostom's contribution to the formation of the Greek Christian mind which, I believe, should be adduced here in connection with the contributions of the other two Hierarchs which we have been considering.

In the *first* instance, I refer to his profound conviction that there is an inner, divinely ordained bond between the natural and the moral order. Here we discern the powerful influence on St John Chrysostom's thought of the Old Testament teaching that a covenanted economy of righteousness and grace undergirds and stamps the whole creation. The temporal order of things is harnessed to eternal ends which come to their focus in God's will for man whom he created for communion with himself. It is in the existence and life of man as a physical and spiritual being that natural law and moral law overlap, and in the destiny of man, therefore, that the true purpose and ultimate meaning of the world will be disclosed.

Christian tradition from the very beginning rejected the pagan Greek concept of *accident*, or of *chance* as a kind of blind necessity operating without purpose. In the doctrine of creation out of nothing, which we have already discussed, Christians replaced the notion of irrational accident or blind chance by the concept of contingence, for they believed that, while things freely happen in the created world which did not need to happen, and which might not have happened at all, they nevertheless happen within the economy of God's providential over-ruling of all things in accordance with his Wisdom, Truth and Righteousness.

The term "economy", frequently used by John Chrysostom in this sense, refers to the fact that the natural order is unceasingly contingent on God in such a way that he not only upholds and sustains it in its creaturely reality, but makes its coherent arrangement serve his supreme purpose in the communion of the creation with the Creator. The natural order, therefore, is to be regarded, not simply as the actual order in which things happen to be arranged, but rather as the kind of order in which things ought to be arranged under the imperative of God's Wisdom and Will. This deletion of the notion of accident or chance by the Christian concept of contingent order under God, carried with it the idea of an overall moral perspective in which the good is blessed and evil falls under judgment.

This way of regarding the natural order and the moral order, as linked together under the overarching Wisdom and Righteousness of God, characterised all St John Chrysostom's preaching. The message which he was tireless in proclaiming in intensely practical ways had a far-reaching effect upon the pagan Greek mind, calling for radical moral change into the kind of mind that looks upon the world as governed, not by blind chance and inexorable fate, but by God's loving and saving purpose for every human being, and indeed for the whole of creation. In other words, here we find taking place a transformation of the Greek mind, as an impersonal, naturalistic, fatalistic outlook upon human affairs yields to a thoroughly teleological outlook of a hitherto unheard-of intimacy, in which God is believed to care intensely for each person and all that happens to him or her in life and death.

In the *second* instance, I wish to refer to what I propose to call St John Chrysostom's "biblical mind". None of the Church Fathers, Greek or Latin, has given us such exhaustive and careful interpretation of the Holy Scriptures, and none has had such a lasting impact upon others through his expositions and commentaries. I need only refer again to John Calvin who was immensely indebted to Chrysostom in this respect and who like him has left a host of commentaries which explain the precise meaning of the biblical texts in ways we can still appreciate and approve. It was John Chrysostom's steady aim in all his preaching and expository activity to instil biblical truth into the hearts and minds of his contemporaries. For the healed and reconciled mind to continue steadfast in the Christian faith and way of life it needed to be saturated with the Holy Scriptures and be inwardly transformed by the Word of God they mediated. The Greek Christian mind had to be a biblical mind.

The Epistles of St Paul were clearly St John Chrysostom's favourite Scriptures, for it is upon them that he has given us his finest commentaries. It was the great Apostle's evangelical message of the economy of redemption, which in his eternal purpose God had revealed and brought to its culmination in Jesus Christ, that Chrysostom made the centre of his own faith and life and the centre of all his ministry of the Gospel. It transformed his understanding of the moral as well as of the natural economy, for it showed him that in Jesus Christ the order of redemption had interpenetrated the order of creation in a final and decisive way, setting it wholly upon the basis of God's grace. It was above all in St Paul, whose whole being was "in the law to Christ", whose mind had absorbed the mind of Christ, that Chrysostom found exhibited what the Christian mind in Jew, Greek, or barbarian really should be like. But this is the biblical mind which the Hierarch sought to assimilate into his own mind and, with all the golden eloquence at his command and an unrivalled mastery of the Attic language, to commend to others.

The first volume of Georges Florovsky's *Collected Works* opens with a telling chapter on "The Lost Scriptural Mind". He pointed out that our major difficulty today begins with the habit we have acquired of measuring the Word of God by our own stature, instead of checking our mind by the stature of Christ. He claimed that we have lost the integrity of the Scriptural mind, and thus fail to sustain "the faith once delivered to the saints", in the way in which we ought in fidelity to the truth of the Gospel. Our modern mind needs to be brought under the judgment of the Word of God and to be transformed by the mind of Christ. That is

13

precisely what St John Chrysostom set out to do in his own ministry in Antioch and Constantinople, in line with the tradition that had already been set so clearly by St Basil of Caesarea and St Gregory Nazianzen.

I believe that in linking closely together the contributions of these three Hierarchs to the formation of the Greek Christian mind, we ourselves will be on the road to recovering the Mind of Christ in a way that will be relevant and effective in the scientific culture of our own time. Under God we have been rediscovering the contingent nature of the universe and its open-textured order which point beyond themselves altogether to the transcendent source and ground of their rationality in the Word of God. That is the very Word who became flesh in Jesus Christ, our Lord and Saviour. In him, as St Paul has taught us, all things were created, in heaven and on earth, visible and invisible, created through him and for him. He is before all things, and in him all things consist and hold together. Moreover, it is in and through him that we who once were alienated and hostile in our minds are now reconciled to God and are at peace with him. With minds inwardly transformed and sanctified in Christ, we may look in new light upon the whole universe of space and time, with its astonishing order and beauty daily being disclosed by our science, as the theatre of God's self-revelation and the sanctum for our worship and praise of the Creator and Redeemer.

REFERENCES

St Athanasius,
Against the Arians, The Nicene and Post-Nicene Fathers, vol.IV.
Against Apollinaris, in *Later Treatises of Athanasius*, Library of the Fathers.

St Basil,
Hexaemeron, The Nicene and Post-Nicene Fathers, vol.VIII.

St John Chrysostom,
Commentaries on the Epistles of St Paul, Library of the Fathers.

St Gregory Nazianzen,
Letters to Cledonius, The Nicene and Post-Nicene Fathers, vol.VII.

George Dragas,
"St Basil's Doctrine of Creation", *EKKLESIA kai THEOLOGIA*, vol.3, 1982, pp.1097-1132.

Georges Florovsky,
"The Concept of Creation in Saint Athanasius", *Studia Patristica, 1962, pp.36-57.*
"The Lost Scriptural Mind", *Collected Works*, vol.I.

Methodios Fouyas,
"The Social Message of John Chrysostom", in *THEOLOGIKAI kai HISTORIKAI MELETAI. SYLLOGE DEMOSIEYMATON.* Tomos Hektos, pp.9-167.

T.F.Torrance,
Theology in Reconciliation, 1975.

Chapter 2

THE CONCEPT OF ORDER IN THEOLOGY AND SCIENCE

All rational knowledge has to do with order, in developing an orderly account of the way in which things actually are in their own inherent structure or intelligibility. If they were not orderly in themselves they would not be intelligible to us and would not be open to rational description and explanation. Broadly speaking, then, we are accustomed to equate the orderly with the rational, and the disorderly with the irrational or at least the non-rational. It should be noted right away, however, as Alastair McKinnon has shown so clearly, that order is not something that we can ever prove, for we have to assume order in any attempt at proof or disproof. That is to say, order presupposes an ultimate ground of order, with which we operate at the back of our mind in all rational activity. Belief in order, the conviction that, whatever may appear to the contrary in so-called random or chance events, reality is intrinsically orderly, constitutes one of the ultimate controlling factors in all rational and scientific activity. The same belief in order, together with a refusal to accept the possibility of an ultimate fortuitousness behind the universe, lies deeply embedded in religious consciousness. Where is that more powerfully expressed than in the anguished cries of the Old Testament Psalmists whose faith in the truth, righteousness and steadfast love of God remains finally unshaken in spite of being desperately baffled by the frequent triumph of evil in the world?

Thus both the scientific and the religious approaches to states of affairs that defy rational explanation do not make us abandon our belief in order. They point us to an ultimate ground of order both as a sufficient reason for our compulsive belief in order and as a controlling centre of reference for a scientific or a theological interpretation of what would otherwise appear quite disorderly and irrational. This ultimate ground of order is and must be hidden, for in the nature of the case it cannot be conceptualised far less explained in terms of the orderly arrangement of things within the universe that is indebted to it. In a strange way it is known only in not being known, or known only in an implicit or subsidiary way as the comprehensive presupposition for the understanding of any or all order whatsoever. Without it everything would finally be meaningless and pointless.

It is the argument of the discussion that follows, however, that science and theology are each dedicated in their own way, not only to clarifying and understanding order, but to achieving order, not only to probing into and disclosing the order of things as they actually are, but the actualising or realising of order in our interaction with nature and with one another. That is to say, in theology and science alike, we are concerned with *the kind of order that ought to be*, through relating actual order to the ultimate controlling ground of order from which all order proceeds.

Let us first consider *theology*.

The belief in order, with which we have so much to do in Christian life and thought, has its ground in the *Love of God*, for it is ultimately God's Love which is the power of order in created existence. Here we are concerned not only with belief in the order inherent in the empirical universe as it becomes disclosed to us through our scientific inquiries, but with the *kind* of order that *ought* to be actualised within the universe, for that is the law of God's Love *for* the universe.

God *is* Love, for Love is the self-determining form of God's Being within himself as God, and therefore also the determining basis of all reality other than God and contingent upon him. This does not mean that God is necessarily related to the world, for it was out of his overwhelming, overflowing love that he freely and ungrudgingly brought the world into being, giving it a genuine reality of its own though utterly utterly differentiated from himself. Moreover he continues freely and un-grudgingly to sustain it in being through relation to himself, thereby constituting himself in his Love as its true determining end. God is the only One who is what he does and does what he is, so that the very Love that God eternally is in himself and in his relation to the universe he has made bears in a commanding ontological way upon it. That is the ultimate ground for its created order as well as its created being, but it is a commanding ground which is as such the ultimate judge of all disorder and evil wherever it may arise. That is why in the Old Testament, for example, the majestic I AM of God is revealed as the one ground upon which all the prohibitions in the Decalogue rest, disorderly ways of behaviour being the very antithesis of what God is, and why the commandment to love our neighbour as ourselves is intrinsically bound up with the supreme commandment to love the Lord our God with all our heart, and all our soul and all our mind, and with all our strength, as Jesus reiterated in the Gospel. The kind of order that ought to be realised in the world is the law of God's Love.

This is the concept of order which Christian theology seeks to think out by relating the Incarnation of the Word of God in Jesus Christ to the creation which was brought into being from nothing through the creative power of that Word. It was thus that the all-important concept of *contingent intelligibility* originally arose in Western thought, as the Christian doctrine of the Incarnation had the effect of overthrowing the

Greek notions of the unreality of matter and the divine nature of the rational forms immanent in the world. That did not take place all at once, by any manner of means, for while the decisive, revolutionising concepts injected into the stream of human culture had a radical effect at the time, they have had to struggle ever since with the persistence in our western mind of pre-Christian forms of thought which have come down to us with an immense prestige due to the magnificent contribution of ancient Greece to human civilisation.

Our task now is to develop this essentially biblical concept of order by relating the creation to the Incarnation from the perspective of its embodiment of the Love of God in Jesus Christ within the spatio-temporal structures of our existence in this world, and therefore in the light of the fact that the overwhelming, commanding Love of God has taken precisely this astonishing way of humiliation, passion and atoning sacrifice to realise its supreme end within our disordered world. In Jesus Christ the new order of the Kingdom of God's Love has intersected the old order of our existence in this world, with a view to redeeming and liberating it from the forces of disorder and darkness entrenched in it and renewing the whole created order. It is encumbent upon us, therefore, to relate the *actual order* we find in the world to the *redemptive order* which lies at the heart of the Christian message. In the Christian Faith we look for a *new order* in which the *damaged order*, or the disorder that inexplicably arises in the world, will be healed through a creative reordering of existence as it is reconciled to its ultimate ground in the creative Love of God. Hence, far from thinking of the saving acts of God in Jesus Christ as in any way an interruption of the order of creation, or some sort of violation of natural law, we must rather think of the Incarnation, Passion and Resurrection of Christ, and indeed of his miraculous acts of healing, together with the so-called "nature miracles", all as the chosen way in which God, the ultimate Source of all rational order, brings his transcendent Mind and Will to bear upon the disordered structures of our creaturely existence in space and time. That is the way of his redeeming and commanding love. The kind of order with which we are concerned in Christian theology, then, is creative and normative, redemptive and regulative, at the same time. It is order fulfilling and expressing the imperative of the overwhelming, unconditional and liberating Love of God.

Now let us consider *science*.

Science, natural and physical science, is no less dedicated to order, not only to the understanding of order but to the attainment of order. The kind of order that our scientific inquiries disclose is not only that of past states of affairs but that of states of affairs which are constantly emerging and developing. This is nowhere more apparent than in the way in which we are forced to relate all scientific inquiries, and indeed science itself, to the expansion of the universe from its initial dense state and the so-called "primeval soup" toward an increasingly ordered state, in an expansion from order to ever richer and more complex order. This has been greatly reinforced by the rethinking of classical thermodynamics in application to open systems, in which we discover order spontaneously arising far from states of equilibrium where instead of random fluctuations or chaos we find more organised, higher levels of order.

The kind of order that arises in nature in this way is what R. B. Lindsay in a very interesting article has recently called "entropy-consuming", that is, an orderly movement against the "natural" tendency toward an increase in entropy or the dissipation of order. But that is, after all, what science itself is, an entropy-consuming activity, geared into the entropy-consuming activity of nature, and dedicated to the understanding and maintaining of order in face of the "natural" inclination of nature to degenerate into states of disorder — the sort of thing that every gardener knows only too well! It is in the biological, anthropological and sociological sciences, in which we study life-processes in various forms, that we find most evident the kind of order that consumes entropy. Indeed an instructive history of human civilisation could be written from this very point of view, as the increasing development and cultivation of order in man's interaction with the intelligible universe around him, in the course of which science in various forms plays an essential and supreme role, as an entropy-consuming pursuit. At the same time, of course, achievements of this kind have to pay the penalty of a considerable dissipation of energy, or the transmutation of energy from an available to a non-available form.

It should now be apparent that in natural science we strive to grasp, not only how things as a matter of fact are found to be arranged in nature, but how things *ought* to be arranged. In our engagement in scientific activity we respond to an ontological imperative which we share with the whole universe of created reality in its constant expansion toward maximum order. Only relatively few people, of course, are passionately committed to scientific research in unravelling the immanent secrets of nature, but scientific activity after all, as Einstein used to point out, is only a refined form of our normal, rational behaviour in the world. Hence it is justifiably to be claimed that the inner compulsion which prompts and drives our science is no more than an extension of the rational compulsion under which we human beings live our daily life.

This inner compulsion is what R. B. Lindsay has called *"the thermodynamic imperative"* which, in line with the second law of thermodynamics, he defines in these terms: "While we *do* live we ought always to act in all things in such a way as to produce as much order in our

19

environment as possible, in other words to maximize the consumption of entropy." This helps us to appreciate why science is always generating fresh and more sophisticated technologies, ways of transmuting available energy into higher and more complex patterns, through which the inherent forces of nature are encouraged to function in accordance with their own latent potentialities for order. It should be added, however, that this thermodynamic imperative is not to be associated with a masterful ambition in human beings to triumph over nature, or to impose their own egos and wills upon their environment in the most convenient way to serve their interests, although, admittedly, human selfishness and greed do actually lead people to misuse science and technology in just that way.

I believe that we must discern behind this imperative to increase the degree of order whether in nature or in human life, something much more compelling, a requirement or obligation emanating from the *ultimate ground of all order* and echoed by the claims of created reality upon us. This is the imperative of which we are acutely aware as we tune our minds as faithfully as possible to the intrinsic structures of the universe, for it generates in us what has been called, very appropriately, the *scientific conscience*. In other words, it is an imperative which the scientist *as scientist* cannot in rational conscience disregard or disobey, but to which he is, precisely as rational scientist, wholly committed. This is what lies at the back of the fact that the order inherent in the universe, which presses ineluctably upon our minds in all inquiry, is a feature of the universe which, as we have already noted, it is impossible to prove but which must be presupposed in all proof: it is the order that provokes and guides our inquiries, on which we rely in all testing of evidence, or in formulating our theories, and to which we appeal in the last resort as the ultimate judge of the truth or falsity of our understanding, concepts and explanations. It is this ultimate order, the ontic truth of things to which we are rationally committed and over which we have no control, which stands guard over all our scientific inquiries and theories from discovery to verification.

Here let me offer three remarks about the ground we have covered so far.

(1) We have now moved beyond the old idea that natural science is concerned only with the *how* and not with the *why*, that is, with mechanical processes and not with ends, whereas theology is concerned only with *why-questions*, that is, questions about beginnings and ends. That sharp distinction had the effect of importing a deep split between science and theology, and indeed between the natural sciences and the humanities, from which our way of life and thought has suffered severely in the most sensitive areas of human culture. It is now evident, however, that the *how* questions and the *why* questions cannot be finally separated, and that they appear different when they are found linked together.

20

I think here particularly of the place that *time* has come to occupy at basic points in scientific inquiry and theory, in respect of the age of the universe, the dynamic states of matter, or the history of atoms and the structure of molecules, and, in view of the unceasing expansion of the universe, the place of *time* as an essential factor in physical law. That time is a central, constitutive ingredient in our understanding of the universe, tells us that the universe must be regarded as finite in space and time, which forces us to ask questions about its beginning and its end, even on the level of natural scientific inquiry. But when in the midst of such inquiries the question *why* is raised, it has the effect of bringing theological science and natural science into closer relation to one another, if only through some rapprochement of their different objectives or ends.

(2) The fact that natural and theological science both operate under the constraint of an ultimate ground of order, which will not allow a divorce of actual order from the order that ought to be, shows us that there is only one rational order pervading the entire universe. Although this may take various forms, such as we have to express in terms of number-rationality, word-rationality, organismic rationality, or aesthetic rationality, they are all deeply interlocked. Distinctive differences and basic unity have to be taken into account in each field of inquiry, but under the constraint of the ultimate order of things over which we have no control and to which we owe obedience as something rationally imperative. To take this imperative seriously will not allow us to segregate in some Kantian fashion a categorical imperative that obtains in the moral realm but is not bound up intelligibly with the ontology of the created universe; nor will it allow us to segregate a categorical imperative that obtains in the structures of created being but is not bound up intelligibly with transcendent obligations. That is to say, we are forced to rethink moral laws in terms of their intrinsic ontological grounds, and to rethink physical laws in terms of their contingent relations to a stable ground of intelligibility beyond themselves.

(3) There is a fundamental harmony between the "laws of the mind" and the "laws of nature", that is, an inherent harmony between how we think and how nature behaves independently of our minds. This is nowhere more evident than in the relation between mathematics and physics, a point that constantly provoked wonder from James Clerk Maxwell and Albert Einstein. Eugene Wigner of Princeton has expressed this in our own day by what he has called "the unreasonable effectiveness of mathematics in the natural sciences". In one sense, the theoretical concepts and structures that we employ are "free creations" of our minds, free in the sense, however, as Einstein argued, that they are not logically derived like necessary deductions; but they are not free in a more basic sense, for they arise in our minds under the compelling demands of

21

reality, to which we ourselves belong in mind as in body. The more profoundly our understanding penetrates into the created universe, the more clearly and fully that "pre-established harmony" between mind and nature becomes manifest, between the way we think and what we think about.

In view of these developments we should not be surprised at the claim that there are deep interrelations between the sciences, between various ways of understanding the universe in accordance with its inherent modes of order, all of which overlap and interpenetrate each other. Nor should we be surprised that this applies no less to the interrelations of *theological science* and *natural science*, although they are concerned in different ways with the kind of intelligible order inherent in the created universe. Natural science, of course, is concerned to explore and account for the on-going processes in nature in their *autonomous* structures, that is, in their contingent reality as utterly *different from* the transcendent Reality of God. Theological science is concerned to understand and interpret states of affairs and events in the created universe, in so far as they are *dependent upon* God the Creator and Redeemer, and are specifically correlated to his revealing and saving purpose in history. But since both natural science and theological science operate within the same framework of space and time, which is the carrier of all our creaturely rationality, their inquiries cannot but overlap, even though they move in different directions owing to the different ends they have in view. And yet the more rigorous their questioning is, the more aware they are of the limits which they cannot rationally cross and the more ready they are to suspend judgment, and even to call for help from one another before the face of the Creator.

It is a highly interesting situation of this kind which we have now reached in our sub-atomic particle research. The way in which quanta behave in our interaction with them is very baffling, for it resists precise description within the parameters of geometrically defined space and time to which we have been accustomed in atomic theory, so that, apparently, only an indirect account can be offered which has built into its basic equations the role of the observer. But then the question is raised as to whether our traditional impersonal understanding of physical reality should not be radically revised, for in actual fact there may be no reality in the universe which is not observer-conditioned! At this juncture absolutely fundamental epistemological questions are posed which physics cannot resolve alone, without engaging in dialogue at the deepest level with other sciences. It is not just that physics has found its limits, but that physics has gained a profound insight into the contingent nature of rational order which it cannot adequately grasp from its own restricted perspective, and where it needs help from beyond its own frontiers. Moreover, the more deeply scientific inquiry penetrates down to the rock-bottom structures of nature, such as *quarks*, which are not self-explainable, it seems to be putting its finger upon the very edge between being and nothing, existence and creation, establishing contact with a state of affairs the intelligibility of which calls for a sufficient reason beyond itself. That is to say, quantum theory has the effect of forcing out into the open the contingent nature of physical reality in such a way as to make a genuine doctrine of creation pertinent in its own field.

How are theologians to react to this turn of events? Certainly the more theologians have the courage to think out the profound interconnections between the Incarnation and the creation, the more they will be forced to regard the startling patterns disclosed by scientific research in the space-time universe as constituting in its contingent rational order a *"created correspondence"* (Karl Barth's expression) to the uncreated Rationality of God himself. This will involve rather more than courage, however. It will mean that theologians must be prepared for the kind of hard intense thinking to which physicists are accustomed, if they are to partner them in any way at these exciting points in the advance of scientific knowledge. The rewards for both theology and physics in this kind of partnership will surely be very valuable, if only in the discovery that there is and always has been a hidden traffic of ideas of surprising significance for both physics and theology.

Now the fact that there are deep interrelations between natural scientific and theological inquiry means that the advantages and disadvantages, the truths and errors, in one inquiry are liable to affect the other inquiry. That there have been such interrelations between theological science and natural science which have influenced the course of each inquiry very profoundly is evident from the way in which the notions of *contingence* and *inertia* have arisen and played a very far-reaching role in modern science.

Let us turn first to the concept of *contingence* which, as we know from an examination of the history of western thought, has a basically Christian source. This is not at all the ancient Greek notion of 'accident' or 'chance' which was contrasted to the orderly and rational, the necessary and the timeless or the eternal, as something essentially disorderly and irrational. In relating the Incarnation of the *Logos* to the creation, however, Christian thinkers came up with the idea that the whole universe in matter and form is created out of nothing, just as man himself, body and mind, is created out of nothing. For the pagan Greek mind that was an impious doctrine, since it implied that the eternal divine forms immanent in the cosmos were created out of nothing, and it was rejected as a form of atheism.

Nevertheless, it was this Christian concept of contingent form, contingent intelligible order, that was eventually to become the ultimate

23

foundation upon which our empirical and theoretical science were to rest. It is because nature is contingent that we cannot read off its rational order though logico-deductive operations merely after the pattern of Euclidean geometry, but may discover the kind of rational order embedded in nature only through asking nature to *reveal itself* to us. This is what we do through scientific experiments, when we put questions to nature in the physical mode appropriate to it, and get back answers which we could not obtain otherwise. Moreover, because nature is contingent not only in its matter but in its form or order, the kind of science we need for our understanding of it must be formal or theoretical as well as empirical.

The problem was precisely how to relate the empirical to the theoretical: how to grasp the actual way in which empirical and theoretical elements are found wedded together in nature, and how, therefore, to understand the way they must be brought together in the structure of science itself if it is to go on being successful. That was a much more difficult problem than modern science at first realised, blinded no doubt by the astonishing advances in scientific knowledge of the universe achieved by Newton. A more satisfactory answer to the problem was given by Michael Faraday and James Clerk Maxwell, both of whom were deeply influenced by the Christian doctrine of creation in thinking out a way to express "the real modes of connection" in nature in the face of the failure of Newtonian mechanical connections to explain the electromagnetic field. But it was left to Einstein to show, especially through the theory of general relativity, how the Newtonian way of relating geometry and experience had to be replaced by another, in which the theoretical and the empirical interpenetrate one another in nature and correspondingly in the structure of science.

Here, then, we have a basic concept thrown up by Christian theology that has played an all-important role in natural science. Contingent order or intelligibility is a feature of nature that forces itself more and more upon our scientific inquiry, in the realisation that order is not self-explanatory, not self-sufficient, not timeless or necessary, but order that is dependent on an ultimate rational ground beyond, with reference to which the created order is the kind of order that it actually is and ought to be: contingent, open-structured order, ever reaching beyond what we can grasp or define within the four corners of our propositions or equations. This is constantly impressing itself upon us in the altogether surprising character of the universe, and correspondingly in the surprising turns that are taken in scientific theory.

Now let us consider the other concept mentioned above, that of *inertia*. It is not difficult to trace its source either, in late Patristic and mediaeval theology — not to mention Neoplatonic and Arabian thought — particularly as the doctrine of the immutability and impassibility of God

24

became tied up with the Aristotelian notion of the *unmoved mover* or a *centre of absolute rest* which was resurrected and powerfully integrated with Latin scholastic philosophy, science and theology. In theology itself, it induced a deistic disjunction between God and the world, which scholastic thought tried to modify through bringing into play all four Aristotelian causes, the 'final' and 'formal' along with the 'material' and 'efficient' causes. The effect of this, however, was not to overcome the dualist modes of thought inherited through St Augustine, the great *Magister Theologiae*, but actually to harden the dualism by throwing it into a causal structure. This was particularly apparent in the conception of sacraments as "causing grace", which was further aggravated (as in the doctrine of the "real presence") by the acceptance of Aristotle's definition of place as "the immobile limit of the containing body". In mediaeval science, on the other hand, the conception of a causal system ultimately grounded in and determined by a centre of absolute rest had the effect of obstructing attempts to develop empirical interpretations of nature for it denigrated *contingentia* as irrational.

It was, alas, the theological and metaphysical concept of inertia thrown up in this way that was taken up and built into the fabric of western classical science by Galileo, Descartes and Newton, when inertia, used as a kind of mathematical 'x' from which to make calculations about bodies in motion became mythologised into a kind of force. There is no doubt that inertia played a very important role in the remarkable elaboration of a coherent and consistent 'system of the world' within the static parameters of Euclidean geometry, which was very successful within its own limits. The end-result, however, was the damaging idea of the closed mechanistic universe, by which not only theology but all our western culture became seriously infected. The concept of inertia is still proving very difficult to dislodge, in spite of the work of Clerk Maxwell and Einstein, Bohr and Heisenberg, but this is due, in part at least, I believe, to the fact that the cultural framework of thought, within which scientific inquiry and theory operate and are expressed, has been profoundly shaped by it. In this way inertia has itself acquired a hidden inertial force, in virtue of which it continues to obstruct the kind of open-textured scientific thinking required at the frontiers of knowledge. In face of this Christian theology can only cry *mea culpa, mea maxima culpa,* for it was largely through its influence that modern classical science took this unfortunate path.

Today a steady conflict between these two basic notions of order, contingent order and inertial order, continues to take place, and not always below the surface. In the course of this conflict there have been thrown up new ways of thought that are shaking themselves free of mechanistic, deterministic structures, as it is increasingly realised that

25

nature is much more subtle (*rafiniert* was Einstein's term) and flexible than can be expressed in terms of the old couplet "chance and necessity". The universe is now found to have an open-structured, labile nature, which is no less but all the more deeply rational than the older closed deterministic view of the universe allowed. This movement within science, however, has been taking place at a time when our theology in large part is still trapped in rigid Newtonian patterns of thought, and is thus unable to give scientific inquiry the kind of basic help it needs in the fundamental ideas that it must develop in order to do justice to the actual nature of the universe as it is now daily being disclosed to us.

The great questions now being thrust upon our natural science run something like this: Is there a range of reality that does not lie within the realm of what we call nature? Why is it that the rate of the expansion of the universe and the tight-knitted nuclear structure of matter seem to indicate that the physical laws which we have to formulate under the pressure of nature's inherent modes of order are so staggeringly improbable? Must we not now think of the order characterising nature at all levels as radically contingent and as pointing to a rationality that extends indefinitely beyond it? Does the order of the created universe not depend after all upon a divine Creator and his will and order *for* the universe and its open-ended devlopment?

It seems to me that at precisely this point there can be fruitful correlation between theology and science. As the mathematical physicist, John Polkinghorne, has recently expressed it: "Behind the intelligibility of the universe, its openness to the investigation of science, there lies the fact of the Word of God. The Word is God's agent in creation, impressing his rationality upon the world. That same Word is also the light of men, giving us thereby access to the rationality that is in the world." If that is the case, as I believe it to be, scientists and theologians must surely act and think together in inquiring as deeply as they can into the interrelation between the kind of order that is disclosed through the Incarnation of the Word, the creative order of redeeming Love, and the kind of order that nature discloses to our scientific inquiries, an open-textured order that is unable to reveal to us its own deepest secret but can only point mutely and indefinitely beyond itself. Yet since this is an order that we may apprehend only as we allow our minds to yield to the compelling claims of reality, it is found to be an order burdened with a latent imperative which we dare not, rationally or morally, resist, the order of how things actually are which we may appreciate adequately only as we let our minds grope out for what things are meant to be and ought to be.

It is when this order that impregnates nature and pervades the whole universe is correlated with the Word of God incarnate in Jesus Christ, that it becomes articulate beyond what it is capable of in itself, and as such becomes not only a sounding-board, as it were, for the message of the Truth and Love of God in Jesus Christ, but the means whereby that message may be received, understood and actualised in human life and civilisation as perhaps never before.

REFERENCES

R. B. Lindsay,
"Entropy Consumption and Values in Physical Science", American Scientist, 1982, pp.375-85.

Alastair McKinnon,
Falsification and Belief, 1970.

John Polkinghorne,
The Way the World Is. The Christian perspective of a scientist, 1983.

Ilya Prigogine,
From Being to Becoming, 1982.

Jeremy Rifkin,
Entropy: A New World View, 1981.

T. F. Torrance,
Divine and Contingent Order, 1981.

Chapter 3

MAN, MEDIATOR OF ORDER

I

Three great traditions have contributed to the image of man prevailing in western thought, the Greek, the Roman, and the Hebrew. Greek and Roman views of man were both governed, although in somewhat different ways, by a radical dualism of body and soul (or mind), the soul being regarded as but loosely related to the body in which it is temporally imprisoned. The Hebrew view of man, on the other hand, was distinctly non-dualist, for his body and soul were regarded as forming an integrated unity, with man's body as body of his soul and his soul as soul of his body. While these different views have flowed together in our culture and influenced each other, they gave rise to deep tensions which we must try to understand, for they are still with us affecting the images of man we work with in science and theology.

It was characteristic of Greek dualism, widely reflected in religion, poetry, mythology and philosophy, that the human mind should be thought of as a 'spark of the divine', and therefore as essentially immortal and inwardly oriented toward the supersensible cosmos of divine realities transcending this mutable, empirical cosmos. Owing to the innate kinship of his mind with God, it is man's nature to contemplate the eternal ideas or divine forms of truth, harmony, goodness and beauty immanent in the world and inviting the enjoyment of the rational soul. It was that inward passion for timeless form that provided the impulse for Greek art and mathematics alike, but the radical separation between the intelligible and sensible realms entrenched in the foundations of Greek culture at all levels gave rise to a persistent rationalistic disjunction of theory from practice.

It was characteristic of the Roman dualism of body and soul, that the emphasis fell upon the material realm of this-worldly realities and matters of fact, while the impact of Stoic ideas upon the general philosophy of life yielded a sternly practical form of rationalism. The Roman mind was essentially pragmatic, concerned with means and ends or technical achievement, and devoted to the establishment of law and order, so apparent in its genius for organisation in society, in the army, in the construction of buildings and roads, but not least in the struggle for power.

It was characteristic of the Hebrew unitary view of body and soul, on the other hand, that the spiritual and the physical were not disjoined but held to be interlocked under the sustaining and holy presence of God. This is very evident, for example, in the teaching of the Old Testament about religious cleanness and uncleanness in physical life and behaviour, which is so foreign to any outlook governed by a sharp dualism of mind and body. But it is particularly evident in the conviction that God and his people were so closely bound together in the fulfilment of his supreme purpose for mankind in history, that he was not regarded as shut out of human affairs, infinitely exalted and transcendent though he is. God and his people were thought of as forming one covenanted society within the conditions of their earthly existence, while they on their part did not need to reach beyond those conditions or escape into some realm of timeless abstractions to enjoy spiritual communion with him. Integral to this Hebrew outlook was an essentially religious view of man, for human beings were regarded as related to one another and to the physical creation through the intimate presence of God and in reliance upon the constancy of his faithfulness and steadfast love. Hence, instead of religion being hived off into some arcane realm of its own, it became the inherent force affecting the way human beings regard and behave toward one another, and making for creative integration in everyday human life, thought and activity.

There can be no doubt that here we have a conception of man very different from that which obtained in Greek and Roman culture, due to the distinctive Hebrew conception of God which we have enshrined in the Bible. At no point does that difference stand out so sharply as in its contrast to the fact, which on looking back we find so surprising, that Greek and Roman views of man lacked any concept of the human being as personal. Admittedly, the specific concept of *person* is not found in pre-Christian Jewish thought, but the groundwork for it had been laid in the Biblical teaching about God and the interconnection between the commandments to love the Lord God and to love one's neighbour.

It was with the Incarnation, however, that the decisive turning-point came: first, with Jesus' own teaching about God as his Father, and our Father, and about the mutual loving relationship, of hitherto unheard-of intimacy, which the heavenly Father wishes to have with his children; and second, with the dawning upon the mind of the Church that in Jesus Christ God himself in his unlimited Love has become incarnate among us in space and time, participating in our inter-human relations precisely as Man, in order to reveal himself to us, pour out his love unstintingly upon us, and reconcile us to himself, and thus to one another. Subsequently, through intense theological elucidation of what had taken place in and through Jesus Christ and of what he had revealed of the Triune Nature of God, the Christian Church came up with the concept of *person*, applied in a unique way to God who is the source of all created personal being, and in another way to human beings who are personal in virtue of their relation to God and to one another within the inter-personal structure of humanity. Naturally, once the concept of person was launched, it came to develop an independent history of its own, with various nuances under the influence of changing cultural trends, but in one form or another the concept of person has ever since had a very far-reaching impact upon views of man throughout the world.

Before we go further we must consider more fully the pivotal significance of the Incarnation for the radical switch in outlook to which it gave rise. Christian belief that in the Incarnation the eternal Word or *Logos* of God had really become man within the structured realities of our empirical existence in space and time, had the double effect of overthrowing Greek notions of the unreality of matter and the divine nature of the rational forms immanent in the world— and thereby, incidentally, opened up the way for the development of empirico-theoretical science as we now pursue it. So far as the image of man was concerned, it had a paradoxical effect. On the one hand, it dethroned the idea found in various forms, that "the man in man", as Plato called the rational soul, has a natural autonomy or self-sufficiency in virtue of its intrinsic affinity to the divine. On the other hand, with the Incarnation man in Jesus Christ was elevated to a central role and destiny in the created universe and its relation to God, in a way unheard of in Greek religion or philosophy.

Here the Old Testament unitary view of man made in the image of God was considerably deepened and reinforced through the acute per-sonalisation of human relations with God in Jesus Christ. He is the Image of God in a unique and supreme sense, for he is both the Image and Reality of God in his incarnate Person. We human beings are held to be in the image of God in another sense, not in virtue of our rational nature or of anything we are inherently in our own beings, but solely through a relation to God in grace into which he has brought us in the wholeness and integrity of our human being as body of our soul and soul of our body. It is as such that our creaturely relations with God are personalised in and through Jesus Christ. He is the one *personalising Person*, while we are *personalised persons* who draw from him the true substance of our personal being both in relation to God and in relation to one another.

As the doctrines of the Incarnation and Creation began to be thought out in their bearing upon one another, the Hebraic idea that God had freely brought the universe into being from nothing was both strength-ened and radicalised, with emphasis upon the creation of all things, invisible as well as visible, intangible as well as tangible, mental as well as physical, out of nothing. Thus all rational form immanent in nature,

31

including the mind of man, was held to be created out of nothing, and therefore when regarded in itself to be transitory and evanescent and utterly dependent upon God for stability and continuity. On the other hand, the whole universe of created being was thought of as given an authentic reality and integrity of its own, and as endowed by God with a creaturely rational order grounded beyond itself in his own transcendent Rationality. This was the conception of the contingent nature of the creation and its inherent rational order, which was so impossible for dualist Greek or Roman thought to appreciate. Nevertheless, it was this very doctrine that was radically to alter the logical structure of ancient culture, philosophy and science, and after many centuries of underground struggle with the classical paradigms of thought entrenched in the European mind to open the gates for the new world of our day.

There is a another ingredient in the doctrine of the Incarnation to which we must give attention, for it is very important. Jesus Christ was not only the Incarnate Word or *Logos* of God through whom all things were made and given their rational order, but the direct embodiment of the eternal Love of God within the structured objectivities and intelligibilities of our spatio-temporal world. So far as the Christian doctrine of creation was concerned, this meant that the universe is to be understood as having been brought into existence through the free ungrudging act of God's immeasurable Love, and that it is to this very Love that we are to trace the ultimate power of order in the universe. It is within this perspective also that the whole redemptive mission of Jesus is to be appreciated: as the mighty act of God bringing the power of his Love to bear upon our disordered existence in this world, vanquishing the dark forces of alienation, healing the tensions between visible and invisible, physical and spiritual realities, and reconciling all things to himself, thereby bringing peace to the entire creation. That is to say, the Incarnation has to be thought of as the decisive intervention in our midst by the Love of God, the ultimate power of order, not to suspend the rational order of things at any point, but rather to restore it. And so the whole miraculous fact of Jesus, his birth and life, his teaching and healing, his death and resurrection, is to be regarded as the chosen *locus* within our space and time where the order of redemption intersects and sublimates the order of creation, so as to heal, enrich and advance it to a consummation in God's eternal purpose of Love beyond anything that we can conceive.

It is in that context of contingence and redemption that the theological conception of man in his relation to the universe and our scientific understanding of it is to be worked out. Man is the creature who lives on the boundary between two 'worlds', the visible and the invisible, the physical and the spiritual, or what the Bible speaks of as the earthly and

32

the heavenly. What makes man so distinctive is that as a unitary being, who is body of his soul and soul of his body, he spans both 'worlds', and is thus that unique constituent of the universe whereby it reaches knowledge of itself and divulges the secrets of its vast range of intelligibility. At this point the Christian view of man has to deal with two sets of problems. On the one hand, it has to find how to cope with the powerful hang-over of dualist habits of thought deriving from classical Greek and Roman culture which continue to affect our philosophical and scientific consciousness in damaging ways, as in the disjunction of fact and meaning. On the other hand, it must have the courage to face up to disorderly and destructive tendencies both in nature and in the human mind itself, which is not an easy task today, owing to the habit deeply ingrained in our scientific tradition of generalising away anything like 'singular' or 'contingent' factors that might obstruct the formulation of universal, timeless, necessary law.

In these circumstances Christian theology must probe more deeply into the interconnection between the order of creation and the order of redemption, in the hope of finding and developing the healing answers that are needed to cope with the problems before us. It will operate under the conviction that since the universe is God's own creation the disclosure of its rational order increasingly achieved through our science cannot conflict with but can only serve the order of redemption. On the other hand, it will also operate under the conviction that since Jesus Christ is the Incarnate Son of God through whom all things were created and endowed with their rational order, no redemptive intervention by God through him will violate that rational order but only heal and restore it wherever it has been disturbed or corrupted. That is surely how we must view all the life and activity of Jesus from his birth of the Virgin Mary to his resurrection from the dead, as the Incarnate Word and Love of God at work among us in *order-bringing* and *order-renewing* activity. The role of man reconciled to God in and through Jesus Christ, therefore, must be viewed as one to be fulfilled, not only across the boundary of invisible and visible realities, but across the boundary of the order of redemption and the order of creation, where his destiny, under God, is to be a mediator of order. As I understand it, this is the task, more urgent and exciting than ever, in which theologians and scientists are called to engage today, and engage together, under the compelling claims of the Creator and Redeemer of the universe.

II

Now let us consider, from the perspective of this Christian view of man and his place in the universe, a number of *unresolved issues* in our

33

scientific culture where further clarification seems to be needed, in the hope that we may find pointers to a new kind of synthesis at a higher and richer level of order.

(1) The tension between personal and impersonal thought

I have in mind here two of my senior friends and mentors, John Macmurray and Michael Polanyi, who are no longer with us but whose books continue to provoke fresh thinking. We recall that in sharp contrast to the Christian outlook upon life and reality which was essentially personal, the pre-Christian outlook in classical times was highly rationalist and impersonal, evident even in its conception of man as cognitive being correlated to timeless form. At first sight, a different view might be claimed for the Aristotelian stress upon teleology in that it appears to make room for purposeful behaviour. However, the kind of teleological movement envisaged was taken from natural processes such as the growth of the oak tree from the acorn, which is after all a necessary process far from being relevant to distinctively personal being. Moreover, according to Aristotle himself, teleological relations are causal and have to be understood within a specific set of four causes answering the questions *'what is it?'*, *'how is it?'*, *'why is it?'*, and *'whence is it?'*. Quite clearly, a teleological relation of this kind construed in causal and necessary terms cannot account for personal intention; nor, as John Macmurray rightly pointed out, can the kind of organic continuity it involves begin to deal with the question of *evil*, for evil always introduces a breach in continuity. It is highly significant that when a form of *entelechy* as a process of natural evolution was reintroduced into European thought in the nineteenth century it fostered a naturalistic rationalisation of personal and moral behaviour.

It must be admitted that, in spite of the widespread change introduced into our human consciousness by the Christian conception of personal and inter-personal reality, the impersonalism of Greek thought and the instrumentalism of Roman thought have become deeply entrenched in our western science. This must be traced back to the revolution in the logical structure and method of science brought about through Bacon, Galileo and Newton, when they broke up the Aristotelian complex of four causes, and restricted science to explanatory accounts of material phenomena solely in terms of the *'what'* and the *'how'*. That is to say, they restricted scientific investigation only to what is quantifiable or measurable. Consequently a hard causalism took over which had the effect, not only of excluding from scientific activity the whole realm of personal reality, but of imposing upon the investigation of nature a severely instrumentalist conception of science which gathered up and outstripped the pragmatic concentration upon means and ends that had characterised the old Roman passion for power in the world. Thus there emerged the deterministic conception of the universe as a closed system of cause and effect governed by universal timeless law, and therewith a mechanico-causal interpretation of man and human affairs which disintegrates all rational grounds for human convictions and actions. That is the background for the power-structured technological society which positivist and Marxist philosophy and science have been trying to force upon the human race.

The problem that this conception of the universe raised for the Christian conviction that personal being, divine and human, is of the very essence of reality, was severely aggravated by the absolutisation of classical physics and mechanics that followed upon the immense success of Newton's *System of the World*. There took place what Michael Polanyi has called an "absurd mechanisation of knowledge" in which the human mind itself is excluded from the field of scientific knowledge, in the mistaken belief that through elimination of the personal coefficient an absolutely dispassionate, impersonal, and exact scientific knowledge may be achieved. We shall have to attend to the relation between the mind of the knowing agent and what he knows later in connection with quantum theory, but it should be pointed out here that Einstein, who dethroned classical physics and mechanics, has shown conclusively that no scientific ideas or theories are ever reached through abstractive processes of the kind claimed by the Newtonians. And Polanyi has shown, no less conclusively, that no scientific discovery or verification is possible without the responsible participation of the person as as an active rational centre of consciousness in all acts of human understanding and knowing. After all, only a person can engage in genuinely objective knowledge for only he can distinguish objective realities from subjective fantasies, only a person can discern a coherent pattern in nature and let his insight into it steer his researches to a successful result, and of course only a person can weigh evidence or judge the validity of an argument in response to the compelling claims of realty, and therefore engage in rigorous, critical scientific activity. In spite of the rear-guard action still being fought against it by empiricist and positivist science, the critical reassessment of scientific consciousness and knowledge carried out by Michael Polanyi, together with his reinstatement of the person in relentlessly objective rational knowledge, is steadily being accepted within our scientific culture. Empiricism and positivism, of course, have already been defeated in principle and in fact by relativity and quantum theory, so that when the rear-guard action is over, we can expect a full restoration of rational balance in all areas of scientific knowledge.

(2) The resurgence of contingent order

Sir Isaac Newton certainly believed that the universe had been created by God out of nothing, and that the mechanical causal order which he found everywhere immanent within the universe cannot be extrapolated to account for the origin of that kind of order. In other words, he held that the universe cannot be conceived as a consistent system of physical law unless it is open to a sufficient and transcendent ground of order beyond it in God. In a profound sense, therefore, Newton was indebted to the Judaeo-Christian concept of the contingent universe characterised throughout by a contingent rational order of its own derived from the Creator. However, Newton's basic outlook upon the universe suffered from a radical dualism between theoretical and empirical elements both in nature and in scientific knowledge, which seriously undermined the paradigm of contingent intelligibility or order, and led instead to a necessitarian conception of causal law. He gave masterful expression to this dualism in terms of absolute mathematical time and space on the one hand and relative apparent time and space on the other, and offered a systematic mechanical account of phenomenal events in relative apparent time and space by imposing upon them the rigid patterns of absolute mathematical time and space. That supplied the basic structure, set out in the *Principia Mathematica*, upon which the mechanistic conception of the universe was erected and developed by the Newtonians.

That view of the universe was dealt a fatal blow when Clerk Maxwell had to abandon Newtonian mechanics with its doctrine of action at a distance and adopt the idea of a continuous dynamic field in order to give a strictly scientific account of the rational order found in electromagnetism and light, and when he reintroduced the concept of contingence into the description of nature. Newton's laws, of course, hold good for large-scale calculations, but the rational structure of our understanding of nature and of physics itself has altered considerably, as in accordance with Clerk Maxwell's equations the rigid mechanical scaffold of the Newtonian absolutes has been irreversibly replaced by the space-time metrical field of relativity theory. Since the Einsteinian revolution the open contingent nature of the universe has become more and more accepted. Einstein himself had shown that theoretical and empirical ingredients in nature, far from being dualistically related, inhere inseparably in one another and must be held together in our scientific explanations. In this case we must recognise, as Clerk Maxwell had anticipated, that if our mathematical propositions are certain they are not true and that if they are true they are not certain, and that the universe far from being infinite is finite though unbounded or open, as also becomes clear when Goedel's incompleteness theorem is applied to the universe as a whole.

Such a radical change in our scientific picture of the universe has much to offer for our image of man today. Not least among its advantages is that it provides a modern context for the development of the non-dualist Judaeo-Christian conception of man as creaturely personal being freely created and sustained by God in mind and body together with the whole contingent order of the universe, of which man is an essential constituent and in which he has a supreme function to fulfil. In what follows we can give attention only to some of the implications which this vast switch in our cosmological outlook imports.

(3) The new concept of law

The concept and formulation of natural law had to change with the recognition that intelligible and physical elements are bound indissolubly together within the dynamic but invariant relatedness immanent throughout the spatio-temporal universe, for that meant that natural law could no more be closed than the universe itself. The departure from the Newtonian conception of law, however, is most evident in respect of the factor of *time*. In Newtonian science time was finally treated as an external geometric parameter bracketed off from the material content of theory or law, much as time is bracketed out of reckoning in traditional or symbolic logic. That is no longer possible in the new world of relativity theory in which all bodies in motion are defined relationally in terms of time and space which, far from being 'absolute' in the dualist sense of Newton or Kant, are real features inherent in the empirical universe.

This new approach to time has been greatly reinforced through the discovery that the universe is in a state of continuous expansion from an immensely dense state of matter. The fact that this conception of an expanding universe is now generally accepted means that the concept of the contingence and finiteness of the universe and its intrinsic order has won the day against positivist objections to it on the ground that it involved singularities which cannot be rationalised away in universal timeless law. It is now clear that if the universe is essentially finite and temporal, with beginning and end, and if the matter/energy of which it is composed has time or history embedded in it, then a time-coefficient must be written into the formal structure of physical law.

The importance of this development may be brought out by reference to the dualist disjunction between *"necessary truths of reason"* and *"accidental truths of history"*, "the nasty big ditch" over which, as Lessing claimed, we cannot jump. That was the disjunction which gave rise to the deep *split* in our Western culture, of which we are all only too sadly aware in the traditional divide between between the exact and the human sciences. It was a disjunction, of course, in which the Enlightenment reverted to the ancient Greek identification of the 'necessary' with the 'rational' in rejection of the contingent as irrational 'accident', and it did immense damage in distorting the sciences on both sides of the divide. Now, however, the situation is very different. Scientific truth, which cannot be abstracted from inherence in empirical reality, is itself found to be contingent, and can only be distorted if it is formalised in mathematically necessary propositions. This is not to depreciate mathematics in any way, but to recognise that the significance of mathematical formalisation lies, not in itself or in its participation in some tautological system, but in its bearing upon objective non-mathematical reality.

In a fundamental sense, therefore, the nasty big ditch between necessary truths of reason and accidental truths of history disappears, while the damage done to them in their separation and antithesis calls for healing. A proper distinction remains between the truths of the physical sciences and the truths of the human sciences, but both are contingent and intelligible in their own way and both resist the imposition of rigid mechanistic structures of thought. Reality at all levels within the created universe is found to be much more subtle and flexible than had been thought and too subtle and flexible to be open to explanation or understanding within the old framework of 'necessity and chance'. In this state of affairs the physical and human sciences are much closer to one another and manifest very significant areas in which they overlap with each other and bear upon each other. It is in that inter-scientific field that man, the rational agent of scientific inquiry, through whom the universe may know itself and unfold its limitless possibilities, has a mediating function to fulfil in coordinating and unifying order.

(4) The ontology of mind

Judaeo-Christian monotheism gave rise to a unitary conception of the universe of heaven and earth which rejected all forms of cosmological dualism and polymorphism. As there is one God, the Creator of all things visible and invisible, so there is one created order, one contingent though multivariable rationality pervading the entire universe. Mind and matter, for all their difference, are equally forms of contingent being with inherent intelligibilities of their own. Since the created universe is essentially one, there are fundamental affinities or analogies between all its laws, even between the laws of the human mind and those of the external world, for under God the constitution of the human mind and that of the external world are correlated in a basic way with one another.

Owing to this unitary yet analogical structure of creation there is a real measure of interaction between mind and matter, that is, between intangible and tangible but equally real forms of being within the contingent system and order of the creation, in virtue of which insight into one form of being may suggest a fruitful line of inquiry into another form of being. Thus it is possible for the human mind, in reliance upon the inner connection between its laws and the laws of nature to penetrate intuitively into the intelligibility embedded in nature and grasp its *natural truth*. By "natural truth" (Clerk Maxwell's expression) is meant not some mathematical pattern detached from nature but embodied in nature, not some abstract form of thought independently developed and then imposed upon reality, but one ontologically derived and objectively controlled by reality. The mysterious interrelation between the laws of the mind and the laws of nature is very evident in the extraordinary relevance of mathematics to the physical world, and helps to explain the heuristic intuitions of great scientific minds like those of Clerk Maxwell and Albert Einstein in anticipating successful theory well before hard empirical evidence could be adduced. Such is the power of the human mind sympathetically attuned to the intrinsic rationality of the created universe.

What are we to say of the interaction between *matter* and *mind* or of the bearing of knowledge of *tangible reality* upon knowledge of *intangible reality*? Certainly what physics does is to bring to light the laws of the physical creation and thereby to establish the general framework in space and time within which all human knowledge, including theology, is pursued. Physics, of course, does not control knowledge of the truth into which we inquire in other fields or establish on other grounds, but owing to the intelligible interconnection of all order within the universe, it may nevertheless offer real analogies which can be used to give us a more distinct or precise grasp of truth in other fields. We are increasingly aware today, for example, of the significant contributions which relativity and quantum theory are in a position to offer to biology. But I would not want to exclude from reckoning the fact that a grasp of contingent intelligibility in some field of tangible reality may provide by way of analogy helpful contributions for a firmer grasp of the intelligibility inherent in some field of intangible reality. I think here of the suggestions that even theology may receive in this way from the physics of light, enabling it to express revealed truth in a form which may be more easily grasped and communicated today.

It must be emphasised, however, that in all genuine interaction in our knowing of tangible and of intangible realities, much depends on our taking the human mind seriously as having *ontological reality*, not mind as some form of epiphenomenal consciousness without real existence, but mind as *subject-being* indistinguishable from the human person or controlling centre of rational consciousness and agency. This brings us back to the contingent nature of both mind and matter, or, theologically expressed, to their ultimate dependence on God as the creative source of their existence and the transcendent ground of their cognate rational order. While mind and matter as contingent are given a creaturely reality, and indeed a creaturely rationality and reliability of their own which must be respected, nevertheless as contingent they are ultimately incomplete and require meta-relation beyond themselves to be consistently what they actually are in themselves. That is to say, while they are neither self-sufficient nor self-explaining in themselves, they have an integrity in their creaturely orderliness which depends on and reflects the eternal rationality and reliability of God's own Being.

There are two important corollaries to this contingent nature of the universe and its immanent rationality which call for attention at this point:

First. While contingent realities might not and need not have come into being, nevertheless once they have come into being they *have to be* what they are and cannot be otherwise. Hence in knowing them we are *obliged* to know them in accordance with what they really are in their own natures and not otherwise. In other words, since contingent realities are not self-subsistent but are indebted to God for what they actually are, they are what they are and cannot be otherwise because of an obligatory relation to the Creator. Their being and their rationality must be regarded, therefore, as falling under the intrinsic *imperative* of God's own Being and Rationality. It is this relation of contingent realities and their inherent order to a divine imperative that invests them with their compelling claims upon us which we must meet in all true knowledge of them and in all our behaviour toward them. Since contingent realities, then, not only are what they are but are what they *ought* to be, a true and faithful account of their laws must reflect that 'ought' immanent in their nature. That is why, I believe, scientists sometimes find themselves ready to infringe natural law as it has been accepted and formulated hitherto in deference to law as they intuitively think it *ought* to be.

The recognition that a proper scientific description of contingent realities and events provides an account not only of how things actually are but of how they *ought* to be, goes far toward bridging the unfortunate gap between natural science and moral science or ethics. After all, if in rigorous scientific inquiry we feel obliged to *know and understand* things strictly in accordance with their natures, in a true and faithful way, it is also the case that we feel ourselves obliged to *behave* toward them strictly in accordance with their natures, in a true and faithful way. Thus true knowledge and right behaviour are both responses to the compelling

40

claims of reality which we cannot rationally or morally resist. This is surely an essential part of what we mean by the *scientific conscience*. If science and ethics overlap at this crucial point, it seems clear that commonly accepted views of science and ethics must change in order to do justice to the double fact that there is an inescapable moral ingredient in scientific activity and an inescapable ontological ingredient in ethical behaviour. There is a proper inter-relation between the 'is' and the 'ought', between being and obligation, which we need to recover today in natural, moral, and legal science alike.

Second. Within the correlation between the contingent rationality of the universe and the commanding Intelligibility of God there arise in our minds basic beliefs or primary conceptions which exercise a regulative function in all scientific knowledge, but for which we are unable to offer any scientific explanation or proof. Thus, for example, under the inescapable obligation which the intelligible structure of the universe lays upon our minds we operate with an elemental, intuitive belief in *order*, for which we cannot give any logical demonstration, but without which no rational activity can be undertaken and on which we rely in all controlled scientific operations in research, discovery and verification. Moreover the contingent nature of that order points beyond itself to a transcendent centre and source of order which plays a powerful if implicit role in the back of our minds in the appreciation of all empirical and rational order. It is hardly surprising, therefore, that James Clerk Maxwell came to rely upon a basic cast of mind, shaped through intuitive apprehension of God in his relation to the creation, as a "fiducial point or standard of reference" in making discriminating scientific judgments in respect of the real modes of connection found in the created order of things and of the tenability or untenability of scientific theories. Nor is it surprising that even Albert Einstein should so often speak of "God" in this connection, in reference to the simplicity, constancy, reliability and trustworthiness of the universe in its rational order, or that Werner Heisenberg should speak of his need to tune into "the Central Order", his expression for "God", if he was to succeed in disentangling the mathematical complexities and grasping the sheer beauty of quantum theory.

That the nature and order of the human mind and of the created universe to which it is correlated are contingent, is an ultimate belief or primary conception of this very kind. It is a conviction, however, that has been introduced from outside into the stock of fundamental ideas with which science operates, through the Judaeo-Christian doctrine of God and creation. Contingence is not a truth which natural science can reach or account for on its own, but which, nevertheless, exercises a heuristic and regulative force in the advance of scientific knowledge and in its open-structured understanding and formulation of physical law. Thus in the

41

ultimate analysis we shall have to leave room even in our most rigorous scientific activity for the openness of the human mind to God, the creative and controlling centre of all order in tangible as well as intangible reality. Without even an implicit meta-reference to God our scientific discoveries will be finally pointless and meaningless. This brings us to our last main consideration.

(5) Meaning at the frontiers of knowledge

We have already noted that physics opens up for us in an orderly way, reflecting the intrinsic order of the universe, the general frame within which human beings live and engage in meaningful activities. But when our scientific inquiries are pushed to the very edge of contingent being where scientific analysis and explanation reach their zero point, the undeniable rationality of the universe disclosed to us through our inquiries will not lie down. Far from dwindling away into nothingness or meaninglessness, the contingent universe demands a range of rationality beyond the limits of what can be conceptualised and explained in explicit terms in order to sustain its inner consistency and meaning. This is the crucial point to which our science has now carried us, in quantum theory, where we have to do with what John Archibald Wheeler has spoken of as "meaning physics" at "the frontiers of knowledge". In quantum theory we penetrate to the basic constituents of matter, electrons, quarks and so-called "gluons", where we reach the ultimate border between being and non-being or the very boundary of being in its creation out of nothing. Immediately we try to cross that boundary through an extension of normal scientific conceptualisation or an extrapolation of physical law, we are utterly baffled, and yet it is on that boundary that we have to do with the initial conditions of nature. Although at that point we have to reckon with an elusive dynamic state of affairs which cannot be subsumed under formal law, we refuse to believe that the circle of intelligibility has been broken, but commit ourselves to the search for what John Wheeler has called *"the regulating principle"* that gives order to what otherwise would appear quite lawless. Hence we find ourselves caught up in an intense struggle for the hidden meaning integrating the foundations of physical knowledge, for the rationality and objectivity of those foundations are at stake.

The immediate difficulty we face in quantum theory may be illustrated by the quandary of Niels Bohr. On the one hand, he asserted that "There is no quantum world. There is only abstract quantum physical description"; while on the other hand, he insisted that in the complementary description of nature there was "an objective description, and that it was the only possible objective description". Most physicists would now

42

agree that at the rock-bottom level of quarks we are concerned with objective reality, but the problem confronting us, evident in the convenient artifice of "gluons", is that here we have a struggle between meaning and fact, or rather a struggle to hold meaning and fact integrally together in face of our analytical mathematics which tears them apart, thereby alienating meaning. However, when it was maintained by Bohr that in quantum theory, as he advocated it, we have to do only with phenomena coupled with our observations, Einstein rejoined that in that case quantum theory does not offer a direct but only an indirect description of physical reality through the way one looks at it in specific experimental arrangements. Einstein feared that the Kantian presuppositions in the Copenhagen approach to quantum theory would result in the loss of objective meaning.

There is no need to discuss here the divergent positions represented by Einstein and Bohr, although it may help not to forget that modern particle physics continues to move steadily in a realist direction as objective physical structures in the sub-atomic world become disclosed, and to recall the point made several times by Wheeler that quantum phenomena have actually been registered by nature without the participation of any human observer. However, it would be well to make two matters quite clear.

First. While it is the mark of a rational person that he distinguishes objective states of affairs from his own subjective fantasies, he cannot cut off what he knows from his knowing of it. As we noted earlier, the personal coefficient cannot be eliminated from scientific knowledge. It is only a person who can engage in authentically objective operations and exercise the kind of discriminating judgments required in submitting his mind to universal standards that transcend his subjectivity. It is failure to recognise this that frequently traps impersonalist and objectivist science in narrow-minded dogmatism. Scientific knowledge involves a free, open interaction with independent reality in which the personal and the objective are fused together in the activity of establishing contact with the real world and elucidating its intrinsic rationality. It is an interaction in which the subjective and objective poles of knowledge are complementary, but in which reference to the objective pole away from the observing subject, and commitment to the controlling demands of that intrinsic rationality upon him, must be given primacy. That is the *semantic focus* within which meaning becomes disclosed.

Second. We recall that in the unitary rational order of the contingent universe, in which theoretical and empirical elements are found coordinated with one another at all levels, an interaction between the intangible and the tangible belongs to the essential structure of the real world. That is why the Newtonian way of correlating theoretical and empirical factors externally had to be replaced by another in which they are shown to inhere internally in one another within indivisible continuous fields of reality. It is through the ceaseless interaction of the intangible and the tangible that richer and higher levels of order spontaneously and steadily emerge, and the marvellous intelligibility immanent in the expanding universe becomes disclosed. Is it not precisely that kind of interaction between the intangible and the tangible with which we have to do in quantum physics under the constraint of the inherent rationality of the universe in which our human minds as well as our bodies share? Of course **we** have to put our questions to nature in the form of devised experiments, but the surprising answers we get back from nature force us constantly to revise our questions so that they become increasingly appropriate instruments for the self-revelation of nature.

Thus it would appear that the kind of interaction which we have with nature in quantum experiments is only an extension of the interaction of the intangible and tangible factors that belongs to the coherent dynamic development of our expanding universe. From the perspective of quantum physics regarded in this way it seems clear that we must think of the orderliness inherent in nature as rather *more sophisticated and resilient* than had been realised in classical mechanics or in early quantum mechanics, when attempts were made to explain and interpret it solely in terms of *indeterminism and determinism*, or *chance and necessity*, which left no room for the all-important concept of contingent order or intelligibility. But is not this elusive concept "the regulating principle" or "the law without law" for which John Wheeler looks?

What startles us so much in quantum theory is that man now finds himself given such a central role in the expansion of the universe and the disclosure of its hidden meaning. For many people today this view of man has been strengthened by the so-called *"anthropic principle"* — an unexpected feature in the expansion of the universe from its originally dense state and in the finely-tuned structure of sub-atomic particles. This has to do with the discovery that in the integrated coherence of the universe in its macrocosmic and microcosmic dimensions the laws of nature are so utterly **improbable**. Thus the universe is found to have expanded at such a critical rate that if it had been infinitesimally less the universe would have collapsed on itself long before any development of life could have taken place, but if it had expanded at an infinitesimally greater rate the distributed universe of stable galaxies and stars as we know it could not have taken shape either. On the other hand, if the inner nuclear force that binds protons and electrons together were slightly weaker, there would be no deuterium which would mean that our sun and most of the stars would not have the fuel to exist, while if it were slightly stronger there would be no hydrogen, and no star at all could exist. In

44

other words, the universe has been so finely balanced and harmonised throughout all space and time against all the odds as to become the universe that it is and ought to be, a home for man with his science and his faith.

Whatever we make of the anthropic principle, it is clear that the central role given to man in the expansion of the universe and the disclosure of its hidden meaning becomes very pressing on the quantum boundary of created reality, where it is brought home to us that this universe of ours is a stratified structure of different levels of contingent reality interacting with one another in such a way as to constitute its wonderful multivariable order. This is evident even in performing an experiment in quantum physics, for while the physical apparatus used functions according to the principles of classical mechanics, the kind of order disclosed through the experiment conflicts with those principles and cannot but appear utterly contradictory and absurd when everything is interpreted on one and the same level. This suggests to me that the paradoxical behaviour of the quanta in respect of time and space is to be interpreted, not so much in terms of the correlation of phenomena with observation, but in terms of the intelligible way in which different levels of reality interact with one other, although, of course, the observational or measuring instruments used belong to one of the interacting levels, while the scientist involved straddles several levels in himself.

It is particularly important to understand that within the multilevelled structure of the universe each level is coordinated with other levels 'above' or 'below' it in such a way that its own organisation is open at its boundary conditions to the one above it, that it is finally explicable only through reference to the organisation of that higher level, and that it plays the same role in relation to the level below it. No level, therefore, is properly to be understood through reductionist explanation merely in terms of the level or levels below it. This means that the intelligible organisation on each level of contingent reality is to be regarded as incomplete and as consistent only through a cross-level reference to a higher and richer level of intelligible reality. But it also means, as Michael Polanyi has pointed out: (a) that the meaning of the different levels which make up the ordered universe is finally revealed by the richest and fullest intelligibility found in the uppermost level, and (b) that the most tangible levels of reality found at the lower levels of the stratified structure have least meaning and cannot as such be equated exclusively with what is real in the manner of classical physics and mechanics, while the fullest meaning is found at the upper end of the scale, where reality is least tangible.

It is surely in that light that we are to regard the central role of man in the expansion of the universe and the disclosure of its meaning, for it is he

45

who occupies the uppermost level of created reality, through whose scientific interaction with the universe at all levels of tangible and intangible reality its marvellous intelligibility becomes steadily revealed. Moreover, man constitutes in himself an ordered but open system of coordinated levels of tangible and intangible reality. Thus he is to be regarded as a microcosm of intelligibility in himself, reflecting and revealing the universe as a macrocosm of intelligibility of which he himself is the crown. Moreover, just as the universe is an indefinitely extended structure, hierarchically open upwards but not finally explicable only from below, so in his microcosmic mirroring of the universe man is in himself a hierarchical system of coordinated levels of reality open upwards but not finally explicable from below. And just as man is to be understood from his relation to God the Creator and Sustainer of the entire creation, so the universe through man at its highest and most advanced level of expansion is finally to be understood from its contingent relation to God. That is to say, the secret of the universe or its meaning becomes disclosed through man's interaction with it, both as man of science and as man of God.

When we push our scientific inquiries to the very edge of contingent being and all physical laws become critical, the need for a regulating principle and for law beyond law, in Wheeler's sense, becomes desperately clamant. A sufficient reason for the multilevelled order within the universe, and an ultimate anchoring ground for that order, are required if the intelligibility of the universe is to be consistent and stable and not to break down and peter out in utter pointlessness. That is the state of affairs which we find at the zero points we reach in quantum theory, on the one hand, where we strike down to the very bottom of contingent being, and in cosmological theory, on the other hand, where we strike back through time to the original black hole or the finite beginning of the contingent universe. What are these zero points, however, but the ultimate boundary conditions where contingent reality is open to meaningful interpretation from beyond itself? In gathering up those boundary conditions in himself man is the one being in the universe whose distinctive existence lies, not only on the boundary of visible and invisible or tangible and intangible reality, but by the grace of God on the boundary between time and eternity, or the contingent creation and God the Creator.

Now if it is to *man* himself that we are to look for help at these crucial junctures, it must surely be to man who is tuned in to the Central Order of all things, to God himself whose Being is the ultimate ground of all contingent existence and whose Love is the power of all contingent order. And yet, strangely, man is the one creature within the universe who straddles more than any other the boundary between order and disorder, for somehow, quite inexplicably, he has become alienated in his mind

46

from God, disorderly in himself and is an infectious source of disorder in nature. This does not mean that man is deprived of his central role in the created universe, but rather that he may mediate order only as he himself is reconciled to God and healed of his own personal and inter-personal disorder. As the priest of creation he is not a means of order in himself, but can only mediate order from the transcendent source of order beyond himself.

And so we return to our starting point in the Christian doctrine of the Incarnation and of the new order of redemption which it inaugurated in time and space. Only if that order of redemption is allowed to interpenetrate and heal the damaged order of creation in himself, will man be in a position to fulfil his unique role within the creation. He must be man of God as well as man of science, mediating order through participation in the kind of order revealed in Jesus Christ, not by power but through love, reconciliation, and service. If this conception of man's central role in the expanding universe is accepted, especially in the light of the essential place that *time* is now accorded by our science in its understanding of the universe and in its formulation of basic physical law, then man must be regarded as having a very important function to fulfil, not only on the boundary between the tangible and the intangible, or between order and disorder, but between between being and becoming and between the present and the future. In that case scientific cosmology and Christian eschatology must be thought carefully into each other, for the future of the human race may be at stake.

REFERENCES

Ray S. Anderson,
On Being Human, Essays in Theological Anthropology, 1982.

Albert Einstein,
Ideas and Opinions, 1954.

Michael Polanyi,
Personal Knowledge, Towards a Post-Critical Philosophy, 1958.
The Study of Man, 1959.
Knowing and Being, 1969.

T. F. Torrance,
The Ground and Grammar of Theology, 1980.
Christian Theology and Scientific Culture, 1980.
Divine and Contingent Order, 1981.
Transformation and Convergence in the Frame of Knowledge, 1984.

T.F.Torrance (Editor),
Belief in Science and in Christian Life. The Relevance of Michael Polanyi's Thought For Christian Faith and Life, 1980.

John A. Wheeler and W. H. Zurek (Editors),
Quantum Theory and Measurement, 1983.

Chapter 4

THE UNIVERSITY WITHIN A CHRISTIAN CULTURE

Today Universities are in process of changing their character more rapidly than at any time before, and without sufficient consideration of where they are going, of what is happening to them, or of what they ought to try to be in the new world opening up ahead. If Universities are to fulfil their historical role it is imperative that we think out again carefully what a University ought to be and what it actually can be in the conditions of our times.

In order to clarify the context in which this kind of basic rethinking is needed, let us first look at the changes that are taking place, for it is important to understand them and the forces that are behind them.

1) *Universities change under the pressure of insistent social needs and demands.* Response to a changing society is natural and proper for any University engaged in the advance of human culture, so long as the dedication of a University to the pursuit of knowledge in its purity and universality remains paramount. But there are forces at work deflecting the University from its proper aims. Coming from outside there are pressures upon a University to serve social, industrial and political ends. And today these pressures are enormously reinforced through economic stringency resulting from mismanagement of our national resources. Again and again Universities find themselves trapped in a situation in which Governments exercise increasing control over the economy, and thus inevitably over cultural development. This kind of pressure, not to speak of dictation, from outside a University has the effect of destroying what a University essentially is. Inside the Universities themselves, however, there are parallel forces at work seeking to politicise the Universities and thus to introduce into the whole institution of inquiry in a University *ideological slants.* And that again is a severe threat to the heart and function of a University which must be free from all partiality.

2) *Universities are under pressure from the technological development of our human way of life.* This is tied up with the interaction of our scientific research and the innovative society, in which the great industries play a considerable role. Behind much of this lies, of course, certain positivist trends in western thought, such as the dominance of the idea of **homo faber** in an instrumentalist science, or the transference to society of the Newtonian conception of nature as a mechanical system of separated particles interacting causally with one another. But what I am concerned

49

with at the moment is the pressure that comes from a developed technology which gathers a momentum of its own and gets out of control. In yielding to pressure of that kind Universities are tempted to sacrifice an excessive amount of their financial resources, only to find, as so often happens, that they are mounted on a technological machine that runs away with them. Apart from technology, however, there is the hard fact that our scientific exploration of the universe has reached the point in field after field, as in physics or medicine, where we can proceed only with extremely expensive equipment: and that means that we easily become caught in a severe imbalance in the priorities of a University. I am not objecting to expensive science — far from it; but we ought to see that a proper balance befitting a University is maintained, if we are to avoid serious dislocation in academic and scientific activity, such as we get when the pursuit of the truth for the truth's sake, or even the pursuit of pure science, is ousted by the demands of the technological society. This is a state of affairs common to Marxist societies, but increasingly evident in western democracies as well.

3) *There are pressures also from the changing foundations of human life and thought*. Here we have to take into reckoning changes in cosmological and epistemological outlook which affect not only the structures of knowledge but the patterns of our life and culture at very deep levels. It is a basic shift in orientation similar to that which western culture suffered in its transition from the Ptolemaic to the Newtonian world view. For some three hundred years we have been passing through a period in which we have pursued human inquiry in a severely analytical manner, and on radically dualist foundations, which has resulted in a fragmentation of thought and culture, in a pluralist society, and in deep clefts in the heart of academic aims. It is in this development that one must look at the pressures that come from abstractive procedures, the narrowing of scientific inquiries, extreme specialisations, and the serious collapse of cultural unity, not least between the sciences and the humanities.

The Universities, of course, have contributed to these changes, and they have given force to the pressures generated as they have adapted themselves to the changes they have helped to bring about in society and culture. But once again we are in the midst of a *fundamental shift* in outlook, far from the dualist cosmologies and epistemologies of past eras, Ptolemaic or Newtonian, to a *new world* in which dualism is being left behind, in which analytical and abstractive modes of thought are giving way to integrative and constructive modes of inquiry and knowledge. At the moment we are in a transitional period, in which the older patterns of thought, still deeply entrenched in the pursuit of knowledge, especially in the social sciences, are breaking up under changes in the depths as, for example, the implications of relativity theory work themselves out in the epistemological structures of inquiry in field after field. The fragmentation of our cultural patterns, the widespread confusion in many areas of knowledge, the struggle of interdisciplinary activities to establish themselves in academic societies, are all symptoms of the break-up of old rigid and positivist ways of thought; but the shape of things to come is only beginning to emerge in the form of open structures of thought and an open society. In these circumstances the need for fresh thought as to what a University is is urgent. How are Universities to cope with the disintegrating forces we inherit from the past, and how are they to function as they seek to measure up to the new world that lies ahead?

In developing an idea of what a University is and ought to be in this state of affairs, let me set forth *two negative considerations*, and then proceed to *three positive considerations*.

Negative considerations

1) A University is not a sort of higher grade school, a glorified high school, at the culmination of our educational system, and therefore an institution to come under the control of the State or a government-established Department of Education. The fundamental ethos of a University is different from that of a school. In a school instruction and learning are the prime functions of teacher and pupil, and the objective is some prescribed standard level of knowledge and competence in various subjects. In a University, on the other hand, all this plays only a subsidiary role, for the prime task of the student is to engage in inquiry, and to learn as he pursues his inquiry under the ultimate authority not of the University teachers but of the truth itself. Correspondingly, the University lecturer is not an exalted school-teacher but himself or herself a thinker and researcher to whom the student is, as it were, apprenticed in academic and scientific inquiry.

If this is so, the question must be asked, whether modern Universities under external pressures are forced into being little more than factories for continuing the educational system and developing certain defined educational products. Universities certainly have an educational function — they give instruction and impart knowledge — but that is of second-order importance compared to their essential functions of scientific and scholarly inquiry, where the governing factor is an absolute commitment to the truth. We must ask, therefore, whether the pressures of teaching in a modern University have been allowed to throw into imbalance other functions that are utterly essential to a University being what it ought to be.

2) A University is not a political institution. The ends are not

pragmatic or utilitarian, although of course if a University fulfils its functions properly there are enormous "spin-offs" for our social and even our political needs. Politics is concerned not simply with human and social need, but with the manipulation of power-structures for certain politically defined ends, and is inevitably biased in a partisan way. Hence if a University is politicised or made an instrument for political ends its essential function would be damaged if not destroyed. It must not be forgotten, however, that a University is a community of people engaged in researching, teaching, studying, administrating, caretaking, etc, and should function as a cohesive body. As such it has an autonomous place along with other primary communities, the State and the Church, each of which has its own independent sphere of operation, and together they constitute the overall Community in which we live and think. Church, State, and University complement each other and function properly together, yet in such a way that one cannot force itself on another or seek to enslave it and manipulate it for its own ends. It belongs to the University to function in this community setting, in relation to Church and State, yet in such a way that it is subordinate only to the authority and objective independence of the realities or fields of reality into which inquiry is being pursued. It is only in this way that the University contributes to the Communities which in their different ways foster it and sustain it, while they on their part are indebted to it at every point where they are involved in the development of human understanding and culture.

Positive considerations

1) A University is a universitas. That is to say, it is a community of disciplined research and intellectual advance in which every inquiry operates through a commitment characterised by what Michael Polanyi used to call "universal intent". Its outlook is essentially universal, and in the proper sense impartial. It cannot be narrow or partisan in its orientation, nor can it serve a limited purpose even if it does function, as it must, in the service of society and humanity. It is a **universitas** in the sense that it is a unitary institution, pursuing an open, universal aim in spite of, and throughout all, the multiplicity of its subjects and interests. And it is certainly a **universitas** in that it transcends any nationally defined ends. It serves the nation in which it is placed precisely through the rational contribution it makes to an outlook that transcends all national, cultural, racial, religious or political division, for by its inner unitary nature and its universal commitment it is and ought to be international and ecumenical. Further, no more than a University can

allow itself to be trapped in a narrow nationalist perspective can it allow itself, if it is true to itself, to be trapped into any narrow specialisations or be dominated by any one Faculty.

2) A University is a centre of cultural life and cultural development. It belongs to its task to carry out, maintain and promote learning and cultural growth, to develop the relation of human beings to their environment in understanding and interaction, in such a way that the empirical and theoretical factors are held indivisibly together. Teaching plays a necessary element in all this, and cannot be ousted by research without serious detriment, for a University functions in a continuity of cultural development and must foster understanding of its cultural heritage and advance within it. But when we speak of a University as developing the relations of human beings to their environment, it is the *universe* itself that we must keep in mind, for it is our human task to explore and seek to understand the universe of which the human being is an *essential* constituent. Indeed the human being is that element within the universe whereby the universe comes to know and understand itself, and through which its inner structures, connections and intelligibilities are unfolded and brought to rational expression. Moreover, since a University is concerned with human beings in their relation to the universe and not with the universe cut off from human understanding, concerned with what human beings do in space and time and with how they fulfil their role in the universe, the whole realm of human, social and historical and, not least, *theological* studies, belongs to a University as of essential right.

3) A University is dedicated to the pursuit of the truth and to the maintaining of the truth for its own sake, so that the truth itself whenever and wherever it becomes disclosed through our inquiries is allowed to retain its own weight and majesty, its own authority and sovereignty over us. Human inquiry has thus a transcendent reference which carries it not only beyond all narrow and merely pragmatic ends, but also beyond the very institutions and traditions which inevitably arise within a University in its pursuit of the truth. It is through this correlation of a University with the ultimate authority and majesty of the truth itself that it is enabled to transcend the limitations of all cultures and ages and societies. And it through that correlation that the University acquires a status that is characterised by a certain majesty and authority of its own, and as such fulfils a magisterial role in human life and culture from age to age. Let us not forget here the enormous place in a University of pioneering research and great discovery — these are what, especially in modern times, shape the character, build the prestige, and establish the real authority of a University. In this respect, it is evident, not a few modern Universities have attained a reputation and a prestige which are comparable with

those of the most ancient Universities of Europe, and not infrequently surpass and sometimes even supersede them, precisely because they have established themselves in a compelling relationship to the structures of reality beyond themselves.

In the *general* characterisation set out in these considerations of what a University is and ought to be, reference has been made to certain *particular* features and functions of a University which now demand of us fuller discussion.

1) ***Rigorous inquiry.*** It has been characteristic of Universities in the last four hundred years that they have become deeply involved in the kind of questions that yield positive knowledge, or what has been known since ancient times as "dogmatic science", **dogmatike episteme**, as the Greeks expressed it. These are not problematic questions, questions raised to resolve difficulties in knowledge we already claim to have, but genuine interrogations of reality seeking answers which could not be inferred from what we already know. They are questions that are forced upon us by the objective or intrinsic structures of reality that come to light in our on-going inquiry. This entails a sharpening and intensification of questioning as we question our questions in the light of what they reveal, so that the questions become progressively freed from the assumptions and presuppositions with which they started, and progressively open towards the fields of inquiry to which they are directed. Not only prejudgments and prejudices but the predetermining force of all external authorities are set aside in such a process, as the mind of the inquirer falls more and more under the power of the intrinsic intelligibilities and objective structures of the realities being investigated. Moreover, since questions cannot ultimately be separated from the questioners, the more relentlessly questions are themselves questioned, the more questioning cuts back critically upon the questioners, until questioned down to the roots of their being they find themselves being laid open in childlike wonder to disclosure from beyond themselves. Selfless inquiry of this kind has a positive character which differentiates it sharply from the cult of scepticism which, as we learn from the "New Academy" in ancient Athens, can only breed sterile "academic questions", and which, as we learn from the practice of systematic doubt in Cartesian circles in the seventeenth century, in the last analysis pivots upon the self-certainty of the thinker and thus does not escape from the clutches of a massive subjectivity. Undoubtedly it is the pursuit of rigorous, positive questioning by the pure sciences in our Universities which has had a marked impact upon the kind of open inquiry with which our Universities have come to be correlated in recent times.

2) ***Freedom.*** There is a structured relation between scientific and academic inquiry and the institutional life of the community in which that

inquiry is carried out. Just as scientific and academic inquiry in any field demands of us detachment from all presuppositions and extraneous principles and authorities, so the community of inquiry must be independent of all external forces or authorities, for any intervention by them would corrupt or destroy the purity and objectivity of the purposes and functions of a University. A University may be regarded, therefore, as the community coefficient of the scientific enterprise and conscience, with freedom from any control other than that which arises out of commitment to objective knowledge. Without freedom of this kind a University perishes; in spite of all institutional appearance it is not a University in the proper sense. The scientific and academic freedom in which a University flourishes is found only under the control of the *truth*, for it is the truth itself which liberates the mind, and it is truth over which we have no control that is the continuing source of our freedom.

Difficulties certainly arise here in the relationship between freedom and authority, but they become problems only in so far as we decline to submit all institutional direction and organisation to the ultimate authority of the truth itself. This does not mean that scientific and academic work can be carried out in institutions that have no framework of authority or control, but that the community in which they are carried out must develop its own system of self-control, one that is consonant with the nature of the authority universally acknowledged in scientific and academic activity. Just as a science needs its own internal checks and a community of verifiers reaching far beyond the bounds of the life and operation of a University through which knowledge is tested and acknowledged, so an academic community requires its own internal checks and system of mutual control among its participants, but one which is open to critical testing by the whole community of scientists and scholars throughout the world. That is to say, the kind of control required in a University is the kind that must arise from within the functioning of critical inquiry, and must be exercised through those competent in the scientific and academic pursuits it serves, and in a way entirely consistent with scientific objectivity. In a University, therefore, freedom and authority go together. The structure of freedom and authority in their interrelation must be such that authority serves freedom and freedom is maintained through dedication to the truth for the truth's sake. Undoubtedly, academic freedom and authority thus envisaged cannot be isolated from the wider society in which the University functions and by which it is maintained. However, although the freedom and authority of this society can be maintained only through the development of certain practical ends, the freedom and authority of a University cannot be regarded as an extension, in fact or in kind, of the freedom and authority of that society. The State may supply the fuel and the funds for the

University machine, but does not control its operation. The University is related to the State much as is the judicial system, in that the State is committed to support scientific and academic activity without in any way impairing their integrity or independence. Hence the freedom and authority of a University are bound up with the absolutely primary place of basic research and pure science within it, pursued in independence of any external pressure or motivation.

On the other hand, this kind of scientific inquiry operating within a University does have considerable effect in the relations of freedom and authority in the society within which the University functions. This is nowhere more evident today than in the U.S.S.R. in the remarkable "spin-off" from their space-programme pursued in such tense competition with that of the U.S.A. Soviet scientists have been forced into stricter and closer fidelity to the rational structures inherent in the Universe in their attempts really to understand them, and develop their own inventions and technology in accordance with the dictates of objective reality, for not only success but life depends upon this, but that has meant progressive detachment from the control of the State and the technological society within which such inquiry takes place. It is as this freedom from external and ideological control has been achieved and has attracted to its support men of letters in such a way that scientific freedom threatens to spill over into general life and culture affecting social and political structure, that the State has been forced to use the mailed fist in order to preserve intact its politically defined ends. It is a situation similar to this, as Michael Polanyi has shown, that one must discern in the so-called "Hungarian revolution" when Soviet might smashed the freedom that grew out of the pursuit of the truth for the truth's sake. Yet ferment of this kind is precisely what is going on in Russia itself, as the positivist foundations of Marxist-controlled science are steadily being undermined, and new spiritual freedom is being achieved in spite of the State's efforts to suppress it.

3) *Stability and serenity.* Without freedom from ends and regulations imposed from without the spontaneity and creativity of inquiry within a University are severely crushed, but without inner stability and serenity the all-important conditions for reflection and genuine advance are wanting. These conditions are hard to come by in the social and economic tensions of the so-called "rat-race" of modern life. On the one hand, circumstances have forced us to develop Universities within the areas of dense urban activity or have allowed Universities once relatively isolated to be engulfed in the tentacled-spread of industrial concerns the profits of which, nevertheless, contribute considerably to scientific research within the Universities. On the other hand, it seems to be less and less possible for young people to regard life and work at a

University as anything other than means for furthering their careers or enabling them to earn a living for themselves and their families.

All this means that the University as a place for free inquiry and contemplation, unruffled thought and meditation, is severely threatened, for the internal life of a University is more and more determined by examinations and their results, and the pragmatic ends of students pressurise them into concern to develop clever techniques for attaining good degrees rather than to dedicate themselves to the service of the truth itself in whatever field they may be studying. Such an internal state of affairs engenders tense conditions between teachers, students and administrators, into which "University politics" makes its devastating inroads. Thus the stability and serenity of a University suffer severely under the effects of academic strife, and of the proliferation of administrative regulation which, instead of serving stability and serenity, tend to develop built-in and therefore inescapable possibilities for continuous conflict. And when, as so often happens, a large proportion of the student body opts out of this kind of warfare, the field is left to the ideologically motivated militants whose activities in our own days have sometimes destroyed Universities. These problems within a University are undoubtedly geared into the economic and political tensions in the society within which the University operates, but they are also in part the result of the present state of some of the social sciences which are too frequently trapped within the cultural split and reflect fragmenting patterns of an anachronistic positivism and scientism.

In these circumstances it is all the more important that we take measures to make the Universities *stable open systems*, detached from the strife and tactics of society around them, where steady, responsible attachment to fields of inquiry engenders a spiritual commitment to truth and where truth is thus allowed to function as a transcendent centre of reference making for stability in life as well as in thought. Academic detachment does not mean detachment from the object of study or the realities being investigated, but the very reverse: such an attachment to them that the student becomes detached from extraneous centres of authority and prejudicial direction. It is in the interplay of such dedicated attachment and detachment alone that students can participate in the fundamental ends of a University and contribute to them as authentic agents in the service of truth and the advance of knowledge. I believe we cannot exaggerate the importance for a University to be a stable, open sphere of inquiry, or the importance for students to live and work in a University of this kind where they can enjoy a quiet, contemplative life and be immersed in an atmosphere of calm intellectual inquiry, in which thinking and learning are coupled uniquely with passionate dedication to the truth. The flowering of the human mind is not something that can be forced, but comes only through steady advance into the light of truth. And for this we need Universities where the contemplative life is cultivated rather as it used to be cultivated in the great mediaeval institutions which gave rise to our European Universities.

4) *Tradition in quality.* If Universities are to maintain their integrity as Universities they must not be afraid of being elitist communities with traditions of the highest quality in academic and scientific competence. That may be maintained only if they apply to themselves, in respect of their teachers and students, unrelenting self-criticism, to make sure that nothing falls below the standards appropriate to their ultimate commitment as Universities. This involves, perhaps above all, a continuity of teachers and research workers of sheer excellence in their different fields, and through them a tradition of authority in intellectual passion and submission to the scientific conscience, as well as a tradition of prestige in universally acknowledged scientific and academic achievement. On the other hand, since a University advances, like a science, through building upon critically established results in the past, it has an all-important educative function to fulfil for each generation of students in gearing them into the cultural continuities of human civilisation, which it does by way of regular tutorials and lectures in a continuous process of sheer instruction. No doubt for that purpose brilliant and outstanding thinkers are not always necessary, so that every University is tempted to make use of "academic hacks", but if a University is really to be a University even this function of informing and instructing students must be done in such a way that throughout it all students are trained to be not mere recipients of knowledge but active inquirers and researchers themselves. And for this purpose teachers who are themselves at work breaking new ground and advancing human knowledge are needed. Thus a University requires a continuity of teachers and investigators of the highest rank, so that through apprenticeship to them it may maintain a tradition of younger men and women who not only are thoroughly informed in the great achievements of human civilisation in the past and the present, but have themselves started to engage in original and creative work as part of their basic training. That is to say, they must learn to share with their teachers in the responsible submission to the authority of reality and the heuristic penetration into the intrinsic structures of the intelligible universe that lie behind great achievements in the advance of knowledge. In this way a University preserves the integrity of its teacher-student relations through which the academic conscience and the capacity for original investigation are transmitted from generation to generation.

5) *Cultural unity.* A University like a language grows and develops within a society, and like a language it gains a life of its own with a real

measure of transcendence over society, providing as such an impartial forum for critical examination, creative reconstruction, and cultural unification in the service of society. Certainly the fundamental scientific and academic inquiries in a University can be pursued only in tension and struggle with the psychological, social and political conditioning of its ideas by the concepts of the society within which the University exists, if only because the language which it employs carries into its inquiries the conceptual and cultural paradigms of that society. However, if the University is to be a centre for the creative development of a society's cultural life, it must achieve freedom from any psychological, social and political conditioning of its thought emanating from that society, and constitute a centre of cultural unity in itself which transcends the tensions and divisions in the community around it. Then it will be in a position to advance far beyond those tensions and divisions, and to open the way for new syntheses reached in its own developments in understanding and knowledge of the truth.

It is here within a University, as we have already noted, that there are serious problems deriving from a deep cultural split between the humanities and the sciences, and deeper splits between instrumentalist or positivist approaches to knowledge resulting from the dualisms of the past and new modes of knowledge resting upon a non-dualist outlook upon the universe in which empirical and theoretical ingredients in knowledge are held inseparably together. These new modes of knowledge turn out to be not primarily analytical or abstractive, or therefore culturally divisive, but rather to be integrative, inasmuch as they constitute a refining and developing of our ordinary ways of knowing and understanding the world around us. They are built upon natural, dynamic coherences latent in the interrelations between man and nature, upon which we depend more that we often know at all levels of human life and thought. If Universities, then, are really to be today what they ought to be, namely, centres of creative cultural unity and progress in the society that sustains them, they must pursue research in *all* branches of human knowledge, and yet in such a way that they open the way for the development of their basic, natural interconnections in a creative synthesis. In a unitary understanding of the universe, of which the University by its nature should be an essential correlate, the main specialisations which are inevitably pursued must be bridged through inter-disciplinary study, so as to allow for the rise of a creative cultural unity within the University as a spiritual whole. As John Macmurray used to say in Edinburgh University, the University must be the place where knowledge is unified, not merely a house for disjoined specialisms, for properly regarded culture is synthetic and total.

Perhaps this is the place of our deepest failure in Universities in modern times — failure to integrate culture owing to the detachment of knowledge from its deepest foundations. This is most evident in the abstraction of the phenomenal surface of our experience from its objective ground, resulting in the disintegration of form which we find in such different areas of our culture as art, ethics, philosophy, and even theology, not to speak of the social sciences, which has made communication and dialogue between different departments of human learning rather difficult. However, while the fragmentation of knowledge and the disintegration of form have been going on all round us, deep below the surface levels of modern culture there are other, integrating forces a work, which hold out great promise for the future. Not a little of this may be traced back to the replacement of the Newtonian notion of mechanistic modes of connection by that of the continuous indivisible field introduced into our understanding of nature, and of the structure of scientific knowledge, by James Clerk Maxwell in the latter half of the nineteenth century. It has also to do with the far-reaching implications of relativity theory, particularly evident in the foundations of knowledge where a remarkable recovery of ontology has been taking place as form and being, structure and substance, are brought together again. Moreover, the universe that now becomes disclosed to us is discerned to have a stratified structure, knowledge of which takes the form of coordinated levels of organisation which are open upward to one another but are not reducible downward. A profound unification of culture now seems really possible through penetration into the economic simplicities in the ontological foundations of knowledge, and through the development of what Michael Polanyi has called a "hierarchy of meaning" thrust upon our understanding of the multi-structured universe as the different levels of our knowledge of it are coordinated through their meta-relations.

Traditionally it is *theology* that is held to have provided the bond of cultural unity. That is now more understandable than for some time, for theology is closely allied to the transcendent ground not only of knowledge but of the inherent rationality of the created universe which since general relativity we are forced, in some measure, to grasp as a whole. Further, it is more and more apparent in the advance of our scientific knowledge to the limits of the contingent universe that some at least of the master-ideas with which we work have their source in the Judaeo-Christian doctrines of the One God and his creation of the universe, including space and time and all things visible and invisible, out of nothing, and of the contingent intelligibility and freedom of the creation as grounded in the unlimited freedom and transcendent rationality of God the Creator. The fact that these master-ideas (the unity of the universe, its contingent intelligibility, and its freedom or spontaneous order) daily assume significance in the basis of our scientific knowledge of the universe, means that modern scientific understanding of the universe is one in which Christian theology is increasingly at home.

This is of enormous import for the inter-relations of theology and science, for theology today may be pursued only within the context of a world increasingly overarched by scientific exploration of the universe. However, it is also of enormous import for culture as a whole, because it is, I believe, through the bridge between science and theology that science itself can be included within a unified culture, and thus incorporated as an essential part of a liberal education. On the other hand, a linking of science and the liberal arts in this way would have a considerable effect in preserving academic studies from being merely scholastic, and research in the arts and humanities from becoming pedantic or trivial. One thinks here of the sad trivialisation of modern philosophy in its loss of metaphysical anguish and in its degeneration into formalistic discussion. The cross-fertilisation of philosophy and science, such as gave rise last century, for example, in Edinburgh University, to the basic concepts which Clerk Maxwell developed in field-theory, would return to the benefit of both philosophy and science. Then philosophy — and this is surely its future — will be pursued on the ground of actual knowledge in advancing scientific investigation of nature, and science will grapple more fully with its ontological grounds in the intrinsic intelligibility of the universe. Then also philosophy and science will grapple together with the question of the sufficient reason for this state of affairs in the unity and intelligibility of the universe which we can comprehend only, as Einstein used to say, at its comparatively elementary levels.

It is surely right here that a proper theology will have its part to play in rethinking its basic contributions to the scientific enterprise in the light of what has become so wonderfully disclosed through modern inquiry of the rational beauty and harmony of creation, and in reformulating its own concepts in a way that may act as a catalyst making for unity across the boundaries of the arts and sciences. Theology would thus play a significant role in the University by serving the re-emergence of genuine **universitas** in our culture, enabling the University to become in a new way a creative source of cultural unity in human life and society.

Certainly the passing of the age of analytical thought, together with the disintegration of culture that went with it, points in this direction, while the emergence of integrative modes of thought and understanding promise already the dawn of a synthesis of a richer kind and at a deeper level than ever conceived before. The conditions are therefore ripe for the Universities to play their full role in the whole realm of human culture, which has not been possible for a long time. This will not happen unless Universities develop within themselves a proper balance in their activities of research and learning in every field of human knowledge. Universities that do not match up to that challenge will degenerate into strange anachronisms.

Yet when all is said and done, it must be admitted that the cultural unity we seek is not something that can be organised. It is something ultimately indefinable and unformalisable, akin to those ultimate beliefs which, while unverifiable and unfalsifiable in themselves, nevertheless are regulative of all our scientific knowledge of the universe as well as of our daily natural experience. Cultural unity is essentially spiritual which, under suitable conditions, can arise spontaneously out of human response to the unity of created reality and commitment to its transcendent ground in God the creative source of all that is. Suitable conditions surely include an indefinite openness to the intelligibility and integrity of the universe and its ultimate ground, knowledge of which continually takes us by surprise, but they also include inter-disciplinary study across the boundaries of all the sciences and humanities which together with theological science comprise the whole field of human inquiry. That is what a University must embrace if it is to be what it ought to be.

REFERENCES

Erich Kahler,
The Distintegration of Form in the Arts, 1968

John Macmurray,
Freedom in the Modern World, 1932
Interpreting the Universe, 1933
The Boundaries of Science, 1939

Michael Polanyi,
Science, Faith and Society, 1946, new edit., 1964
The Logic of Liberty, 1951
Scientific Thought and Social Reality, 1974

T. F. Torrance,
Reality and Scientific Theology, 1984

A. N. Whitehead,
The Aims of Education and Other Essays, 1929

INDEX OF NAMES